CLASSROOM TURMOIL
TO *Tranquility*

BARBARA FRANDSEN

Classroom Turmoil to Tranquility

Heal Our Classrooms
Heal Our Students

Barbara Frandsen

Tranquility Press 2024

For information or to order additional copies of this book contact:
Tranquility Press
www.TranquilityPress.com
tranquilitypress@gmail.com
723 W University Ave #234, Georgetown TX 78626

You may also contact Barbara Frandsen by emailing barbarafrandsen@icloud.com.

Many of these strategies were taught as part of the methodology curriculum at St. Edward's University, Austin, Texas.

ISBN 978-1950481491

DEDICATION

I Am a Teacher. . .

I am a teacher.

The names of those who have practiced my profession ring like a hall of fame for humanity; Jesus, Booker T. Washington, Buddha, Confucious, Ralph Waldo Emerson, Leo Buscaglia, Moses, Piaget, Montessori, and Anne Sullivan.

And so, I have a past that is rich in memories. I have a present that is challenging, adventurous and fun because I am allowed to spend my days with the future.

I am a teacher. . . and I thank God for it every day.

John W. Schlatter

CONTENTS

EMPOWERING
STUDENTS

Man is unhappy because he doesn't know he's happy. . .
If anyone finds out he'll become happy at once.

~Dostoyevsky

RULES

When writing class rules, keep the rules broad enough that many specific behaviors apply. For example, being respectful includes listening, taking turns, participating, and smiling at one another. One class rule may be enough to cover all bases.

Examples of disrespect would be shouting out answers, pushing in line, making rude remarks, and smirking.

The problem with a specific rule such as *always raising hands* is that sometimes you want students to be spontaneous. Sometimes you want them to ask partners for help. Especially in cooperative learning, there are times when you want students to participate without raising their hands.

Keep class rules simple, limiting the number to no more than five at a time. Always involve the students when creating class rules. You and your students may want to consider some of the following examples.

- Follow directions.
- Be courteous to yourself and all others.
- Respect your property and property of others.
- Listen when others are speaking.
- Be ready to learn!
- Give 100% to whatever you are doing.
- Be in the right place at the right time.
- Do your best. Keep on trying.
- We agree to support one another in all ways.
- Treat others the way you want to be treated.

All glory comes from daring to begin.

~Eugene F. Ware

Quantum Learning

Quantum Learning involves meeting the needs of children. It is helpful, when considering needs, to reflect on Maslow. In Maslow's hierarchy, distinctions are made for various levels of thinking based on the physical and emotional condition of the individual. According to Maslow, a student who is concerned with basic survival, getting enough food to eat and a shelter to sleep in, will have a difficult time with higher-level thinking. On the other hand, once a student has reached self-actualization, she will have difficulty identifying with individuals who are struggling to survive. From top to bottom, Maslow's hierarchy consists of:

- Self-Actualization: aesthetic and spiritual focus on life;
- Self-esteem: self-acceptance and pleasure regardless of others;
- Belonging: respect and friendship;
- Safety: being secure, free from attack;
- Survival: adequate food, shelter, and clothing.

In *Quantum Learning,* the authors state that a nurtured child blooms effortlessly. A stressed, unloved child reacts to life from the reptilian brain that controls fight or flight responses. Freedom from concerns for survival and safety, allows the reptilian brain to control breathing, heartbeat, and other automatic systems as it is designed to do. An emotionally healthy child with a loving family usually responds to life from the limbic system, which monitors and regulates feelings. When both the reptilian and limbic systems take charge of appropriate areas, the neocortex that controls higher-level thinking and self-actualization operates freely.

Setting the Stage

Preparing the learning environment is similar to setting up props for a play. Attention must be given to furniture arrangement, music, lighting, and visual aids. By controlling your learning environment, you take control of the learning experience. The comfort or discomfort of your environment can either enhance or hinder your ability to teach and your students' ability to learn.

Comfort

If you sat at a student's desk and chair for very long, you would probably agree that the furniture provided in most schools is about as <u>un</u>comfortable as you can find. No wonder students want to stand up, walk around, or lie on the floor. Not only are the chairs hard, but within each classroom, chairs are usually the same size. In any one grade, not all students will be the same size. Does this make sense? Only if all your children come in the same size!

Some students do well with the conventional desk and chair arrangement. Others benefit from sitting on the floor at lowered tables or studying on beanbags. Some students appreciate standing at tall desks to read and write. However, until your school district sees the value of replacing classroom furniture, you must do your best to create physical comfort for your students.

Perhaps pillows can be provided for students who get tired of sitting on hard surfaces all day. One teacher provided small portable dividers, which students placed on the floor and referred to as their offices. Offer choices to your students. For example, students can work at their desks, at private carrels, or on the carpet.

Visual Beauty

Plants, beautiful posters, and positive statements create pleasant decorations. Look at your classroom. Is it boring? Is it busy and cluttered? Are your bulletin boards ragged, tired, and out of date? What would you do if you were expecting honored guests? Good news! You are!

Keep in mind that some of your students need a calmer environment. Keep one area of the classroom pleasant and uncluttered. This quiet, calm area offers a choice, not a punishment, to students who need a more peaceful environment.

Recently, a second-grade teacher created a Feelings Center in a quiet corner of her room. One afternoon a student threw his neighbor's art away by accident. The teacher turned to the student whose work had been destroyed and suggested, "Zach, this may be a good time to visit the Feeling Center." After crying in the privacy of the center for a few minutes, Zach happily joined his class for the next activity.

Music

Adding music is another way to make the classroom environment comfortable for your students. Research indicates that baroque music, like that of Bach, Handel, and Vivaldi uses patterns that automatically synchronize both mind and body. Plants grow well with baroque music. Scientists report that the same plants shrivel and die when exposed to acid rock music. Music benefits the left-brain student by awakening the creative right brain. The right-brain student who tends to be distracted finds music an effective way to occupy the right brain and allows better concentration with the left hemisphere.

Create a tape collection with easy-to-read labels. Color code types of music to make selections easier for you to locate in the middle of a class. Consider the following types of music to obtain desired results.

Type of Music	Results
Classical such as Bach or Handel	Improves learning ability.
Classical such as Mozart and Rachmaninoff	Helps imagination and storytelling.
Slower music such as Steven Halpern	Helps with imagery and relaxation.
Popular music such Whitney Houston	Provides pleasant music for breaks and activity times.
Upbeat instrumentals such as themes from TV shows	Welcomes your students to the room.
Special effects such as Twilight Zone, Rocky, Chariots of Fire, or Mission Impossible	Emphasizes special moments or accomplishments.

In general, turn the volume up or down slowly. Just as the eyes need time to adjust to changes in light intensity, the ears need time to adjust to sound variations.

If a student complains that the music is too loud, immediately lower the volume as the child watches. Later, move the sensitive child farther from the speakers. Explain the benefits of using music in the classroom. To keep the room tranquil for children who need a quiet environment, provide small CD players and earphones to those who benefit from listening to music.

The Benefits of Brain Breaks

Take frequent breaks and play upbeat music to create positive moods. Let students determine when breaks are needed. The benefits gained from taking breaks outweigh the lost time. Students pay attention to and remember information learned first and last. They tend to daydream and forget information from the middle. It makes sense then, to create more beginnings and endings. A break also furnishes students with time to assimilate information into their subconscious minds. When study time comes, use baroque music to help children concentrate.

Lighting and Learning

Since some students learn better under soft lighting, bring a small lamp, and create an area of the room that has a soft glow. You may even want to use a blue light bulb. One teacher uses blue butcher paper to cover portions of school lighting. Allow students to wear sunshades or visors if they complain about difficulty seeing under bright lights. Those who prefer to read under tables should be encouraged to do so.

Food For Thought

One teacher keeps snacks in her room. She realizes that hungry students cannot learn easily. All snacks are healthy, yet inexpensive. She does her best to provide snacks with proteins. Students, as well as teachers, are free to eat any time during the day and are taught to clean up after themselves.

Water, Water, Everywhere

Doctors and nutritionists recommend drinking eight glasses of water a day. In most elementary schools, students line up one or two times a day to get water at the drinking fountain. Even if you allow your students to get drinks through the day, most will only take a few swallows. Perhaps you, the school, or parents can provide students with water bottles to keep at their desks. An alternative involves providing small, inexpensive paper cups that children can fill and take to their desks. Yes, children will soak a few papers and books!

Positive Moments

Create a balance of work and play. Learning should be enjoyable. What would students be like if they received six to ten positive comments or experiences for every negative one? You will also want to teach students to give themselves positive self-talk. Students can be encouraged to mentally change, *I hate math*, to *I'm choosing to hate math. I can make another choice.*

Physiology and Learning

Teach students that the way they sit, or stand sends messages to their brains. We live with a two-way system in which the brain affects the body, and the body affects the brain. How would students sit if they were excited about math? How would their faces look? Where would they be facing? Encourage students to fake it till they make it. Send a motivating message to the brain by activating the body.

Mice, Men, and Manipulation

In a research experiment, scientists gave toys to mice in one cage and allowed mice from another cage to watch them play and experiment. Scientists assumed that mice that were observing would become as curious and excited as mice with toys. The study revealed that curiosity and level of involvement were high in the cage where mice could interact with toys. However, passive mice remained just that, passive. Most of your students require hands-on learning to get turned on and excited. Passive learning creates passive results.

There comes that mysterious meeting in life when someone acknowledges who we are and what we can be, igniting the circuits of our highest potential.

~Rusty Berkus

QUALITY SCHOOLS

Dr. Glasser, the founder of Quality Classrooms, began his career as a medical doctor. After practicing medicine, he became interested in the behaviors of children and began writing books and articles. He writes about behaviors, classroom environments, and learning. Currently, he conducts workshops across the nation with the intent of restructuring American schools.

Choice Theory

In his work with children and teachers, Glasser applies what he calls, choice theory. The basis of choice theory concludes that all behaviors are internally motivated and are chosen to meet one of five needs that are basic and generic to all individuals. Unmet needs create barriers to learning and personal satisfaction.

The five needs described by Glasser include:

- a need for freedom to move, to choose, to be independent, and to be in control of actions and thoughts
- a need to have fun, to play, and to laugh
- a need for personal skills, power, importance, and recognition
- a need to belong and to relate to others which includes sharing, cooperating, receiving respect, and receiving love
- a need for survival and safety including food, shelter, reproduction, and maintaining the human body

Frustration arises if a student perceives a difference between a need and the reality of getting the need met. This discrepancy often results in inappropriate actions. Therefore, according to Glasser, all behaviors are purposeful. Total behavior includes:

- actions
- thoughts
- feelings
- physiology (body reactions)

Choice Theory maintains that no one loses control; just makes poor choices. As a teacher, you will have occasions to ask, "Are you making good choices?" A good question to ask someone who blames others is, "Whose behavior can you control?" Usually, you cannot control the behavior of another person (or the physical and emotional price is too high) but you can and must control your behavior. Taking personal responsibility is the job of each person.

Total Behavior

Glasser uses a car to represent the steps required to maintain control and make good choices. The steering wheel represents the need, which you, the driver, want to meet. Need drives behavior. The front two wheels represent actions and thoughts. With effort, you can control actions and thoughts. For example, you can choose to talk to someone when you are angry instead of resorting to a physical attack. Although changing thoughts poses a formidable task, you can decide to view a situation from a different point of view. Remember the example from Quantum Learning: *I am choosing to hate math. I can choose something else.*

The back two wheels symbolize feelings and physiology. Although much more difficult to change, the back wheels will follow the lead from thoughts and actions. Using the car model to explore choices encourages students to alter actions and thoughts to correct emotions and physiology. You are in effect, teaching students a way to take charge of their lives and assume responsibility. You are teaching students to choose personal control and to give up blaming others for problems and mistakes.

Quality World

To meet all five basic needs, each person creates a mental picture of his/ her quality world. The mental pictures become important wants for that individual. Although in some cases, what an individual wants may be unhealthy, each desire corresponds to a real need. Each person deserves to have all needs met, but not all wants should be fulfilled.

Everyone carries a mental image of an "all I want" world. These pictures make up an individual's quality world and define what is important and unimportant. If the real world matches the pictures, the student exhibits motivation and interest. If a clash exists between pictures and reality, resistance and boredom manifest as negative behaviors.

Beginning with number one, follow the vicious cycle shown below.

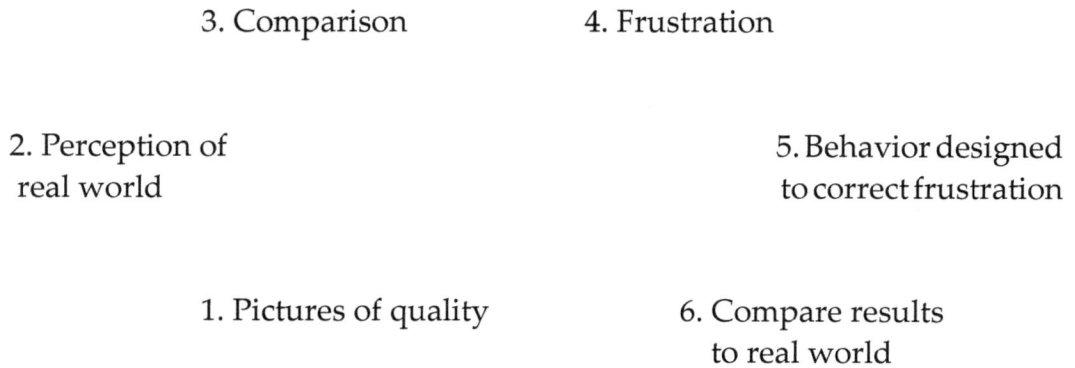

3. Comparison   4. Frustration

2. Perception of   5. Behavior designed
   real world   to correct frustration

1. Pictures of quality   6. Compare results
                                   to real world

If an individual perceives a clash between pictures (wants) in the quality world and reality, the individual continues to act out (make poor choices) to get basic needs met. For example, if a child's pictures of her quality world do not include reading, then everything related to reading seems unimportant.

Behavior, at best, is neutral; at worst, resistant. You will want to do everything possible to meet the real need. In addition, it will be necessary to guide the student to alter his/her quality pictures when they are damaging. Mental pictures are altered through reality therapy questions.

Reality Therapy

William Glasser designed reality therapy as a questioning technique to assist an individual in evaluating behaviors and in planning more effective ways to get needs (and wants) met. The questioning procedure for reality therapy also works well when establishing personal behavioral contracts. Following are types of questions to ask.

- "What are you doing?"
- "Is it working? Are you moving toward or away from what you want?"
- "Do you have a good chance of getting what you want with your current behavior?"
- "What else can you do?"
- "Can you make a new plan?"

Glasser suggests telling students that they take control of their lives by making good choices. Reality therapy eliminates punishment and focuses, from beginning to end, on solutions toward getting real needs met. Glasser encourages self-evaluation and tells both students and teachers that a different choice is always available. The child is choosing this behavior.

Use of Contracts

For a challenging student, you may want to develop a personal contract. When you write a contract with a student, keep it simple. Work on one or two problems at a time. Do not try to fix everything at once. Like class rules, contracts work more effectively and are more respected by the student if the two of you work together. Steps included in writing a contract include the same types of questions and agreements that are suggested under reality therapy and may be included as appropriate. Consider the following guidelines and sequence of steps as you and the student design a contract.

- Develop rapport with the student during a calm time.
- Ask, "What am I doing? Is it working for you?"
- Ask, "Do you understand what I want?"
- Continue, "What are you doing?" If the student will not or cannot name the behavior, state it specifically. Add appropriate questions from Reality Therapy at this time.
- Ask, "Is the behavior working?" Avoid, "Is it right or wrong, or good or bad?"
- Suggest, "Let's make a new plan." Get input and agreement from the student about what each of you can do to change the situation.
- Restate, "This is what you can do. This is what I will agree to do to support you."
- Get and give firm commitments by either shaking hands or signing a written agreement.

If the contract is not working, Glasser suggests using the following steps.

- Accept no excuses if the student fails to keep an agreement. "You said you would do _____. It isn't done". Avoid blaming, laying guilt trips, shaming, and punishing.
- Ask, "Do we need a new plan? What can I do to help you succeed?" Together develop a revised plan with an easier agreement from the student and stronger support from you.
- Never give up!

Notice the sample contracts on the following pages.

Additional Questions from Texas Experts

Jerry and Pamela Webb, behavior specialists from Texas, also recommend using the following dialogue while privately and respectfully talking with a child.

- Request, "May I share something I've noticed?"
- After gaining the child's permission, share the behavior without the use of judgmental words.
- Ask, "Have you noticed that?"
- Follow the child's response with a suggestion. "I would like for us to think about a different behavior. Would you be willing to do that?"

At all stages of the dialogue, address the child with total courtesy. The use of Active Listening promotes trust and a feeling of being respected. Refer to Active Listening on page 45.

Contract

Name of Student _____

Name of Teacher _____

Beginning Date _____

What am I doing? _____

_____

_____

How can my teacher help? _____

_____

_____

_____   _____
Student   Teacher

If tattling is a problem, us a tattletale form similar to the one below to avoid wasting learning time.

Tattletale Report Form

Day _____   Time _____

Place _____

By _____

About _____

And _____

Event or behavior being reported: _____

_____

_____

_____ Another child may get hurt.

_____ I may get hurt.

_____ Things may get broken.

_____ An adult needs to help.

Name of tattler _____

Even behaviors such as rolling eyes or sighing disrespectfully can be dealt with through the use of a new plan form such as the one below.

Alternative Behaviors

Student's Name _____

Teacher's Name _____

Date _____ Time _____

The behavior that is not appropriate is _____

_____

Three alternative ways to express my feelings are:

1. _____

2. _____

3. _____

_____
Signature of Student

Quality School

A Quality School is an educational institution that focuses on adding quality to the lives of its students through education. Students in Quality Schools look forward to coming to school. They feel important and trusted. Quality schools treat teachers like respected professionals. The administrators of quality schools support teachers and believe teachers make responsible decisions that create appropriate learning environments. The core purposes of a Quality School are to:

- develop and maintain quality relationships
- design a quality environment
- inspire students to do quality schoolwork

Glasser offers the following definitions of quality:

- Quality Instruction provides the processes through which individuals discover that learning adds quality to life.
- Teaching is a process of imparting skills and knowledge through a variety of techniques, including explaining and modeling.
- Teachers in Quality Schools are managers whose roles are to facilitate students in doing work that will add quality to their lives.
- Quality is the best action or product that is possible. Quality is defined as the standard that makes individuals feel successful and valuable.

Internal – External Control

Quality Schools create an internal locus of control, which means students believe they hold the power to manage their own lives. In contrast, an external locus of control focuses on external events/individuals as powers that dictate directions for students' lives.

It seems that as a nation, we are experiencing the results of a belief in an external locus of control. Many individuals, reluctant to claim personal responsibility quickly blame and even sue others. An empowered individual who experiences an internal locus of control assumes personal responsibility and changes attitudes and life circumstances.

Lead-Managers & Boss-Managers

Historically, teachers have been perceived as boss-managers. A boss-manager coerces students into shaping up and doing the work. Top priorities include getting students to respect and obey.

Boss managers usually find that when students become adversaries, teaching is frustrating. The boss-manager struggles to get students to work, and students struggle to do just enough to get the teacher to leave them alone.

A lead manager emphasizes the empowerment of students. Mutual respect and student pride in quality affect class goals.

Lead-managers' classrooms fulfill physical and psychological needs with comfortable working conditions. Students become allies, all working for self-satisfaction and quality results. The tasks of a lead teacher are to:

- develop a safe, comfortable work environment
- develop trust
- model quality performance for students
- plan lessons that will fulfill the needs of students to listen, to talk, and to self-evaluate
- remove all fear by empowering rather than embarrassing students.

Lead teachers in quality classrooms improve (at least maintain) the quality of students' lives. The following guidelines help establish what a quality classroom looks like.

- A quality classroom provides a friendly, warm, and supportive space.
- All instruction and assignments are useful and meaningful to students.
- The teacher and the students do the best work they can each day.
- Self-evaluation is encouraged with opportunities to set goals for improvement.
- When students put their best effort into meaningful, useful work, they feel good about school.
- School assignments must never damage students.
- Students can join together and work cooperatively.
- Students do not feel bored.
- Students laugh, play, and explore.

Quality Room

In place of in-school suspension or punishment, Glasser suggests sending a disruptive student to a quality room where a teacher or counselor spends time discussing the student's problem behavior, working with the student to identify more appropriate behavior, and rehearsing new ways to handle difficult situations. The principles and questions suggested in Reality Therapy are used to guide the student to take responsibility and to find appropriate ways to satisfy unmet needs. Although assignments and class work are also brought to the quality room, the emphasis is on guiding the student to make better choices concerning behavior.

Insights gained from counseling in the quality room are shared with the classroom teacher to help the teacher understand the student's needs and make certain classroom instruction and assignments add quality to that student's life. It is probably impossible to adequately stress Glasser's belief that inappropriate and negative behavior indicates unmet needs for surviving, belonging, respecting self, having fun, or being free to make personal choices. Therefore, a major goal of a quality room is to determine the need or needs that drive negative behaviors and to begin to transform the pictures and beliefs in the student's quality world. Until a student believes there are other ways to meet his/her needs, the student will remain stubbornly locked into the pictures and will continue to behave inappropriately.

Do what you can to show you care about other people, and you will make our world a better place.

~Rosalynn Carter, Former First Lady

ENCOURAGEMENT OVER PRAISE

Sometimes, well-intentioned teachers and parents create new problems by giving more praise and rewards than a student can accept. Gushy praise and extravagant rewards tend to detract from the pleasure of intrinsic satisfaction and may create resentment from other students. The student receiving the praise or reward may feel, I'm not really that great. I don't deserve this. Sometimes a student will have an emotional need to show you who she truly is and may revert to negative behavior! The following examples sometimes become burdens for a student:

- You're the smartest. . . cutest. . . fastest child I know!
- You're a great athlete. . . artist. . . writer.
- You are always so sweet.

- You're the favorite!
- You never let me down.
- You're a born genius!
- There's no way you will lose!
- Your grandparents are coming to see your game. I know you can hit a home run for them!
- This A and B report card is OK. Next time, get all A's.
- I told everyone at work how smart you are!
- Everybody thinks you're the greatest kid around!

Honest and Specific Encouragement

When you use encouragement and shift responsibility to the student, the student finds the comment honest and justifiable. Yes, I did a good job on. . . Honesty reduces possible resentment from other students because they see justification in the comment.

Genuine recognition and attention can be very motivating to a student. The following examples suggest ways to give the kind of encouragement that inspires intrinsic values and feelings of worth. Notice the emphasis on the student and how the student feels rather than on what you think or feel.

- You must feel good that you were able to. . .
- Can you see your progress? Good for you!
- That's a good point!
- You paid attention during math.
- You are thinking. You solved that problem!
- You are improving. . . earning. . . getting stronger!
- I think your grandparents would want to see this!
- That's a creative idea.
- You've got it now! You worked hard on this.

- You did a good job leading the science project.
- It's fun to work with you on . . .
- You must have listened well during science.
- Congratulations!
- Let's give a silent cheer for. . .

Alternatives that Encourage Others

The following comparisons offer additional examples of encouragement that promotes intrinsic growth.

Instead of. . .	Say. . .
I'm proud of you.	You must feel good about …
You're my favorite!	One thing I love about you …
This is too hard for you.	Give it a try.
Hit a home run!	Have fun playing ball.
Stop it!	Do _____ instead of _____.
Stop whining.	Use a negotiating voice.
Grow up!	Yes, this is a stretch.
Be a good boy.	Be responsible for yourself.
Shame on you.	We all make mistakes.
You're driving me crazy!	Please scream outside.
Be careful. Don't. . .	Take care of yourself.
Let me tell you.	Would you like a new idea?
Let me fix it for you.	How about some help?
Next time, get all A's.	You seem to enjoy learning.
Nice girls don't say that.	Thanks for sharing your feelings.

Instead of referring students to the office for problems or sending complaints home to parents, consider a positive referral such as the one below.

Referral for Recognition

Date _____ Time _____

To _____
_____ parent _____ principal _____ other

About _____

Who earned recognition by:

_____ helping others

_____ organizing materials

_____ thinking

_____ working in a group

_____ working independently

_____ writing

_____ reading

_____ doing math

_____ other: _____

Expect the best and you're likely to get it.

DIFFERENTIAL REINFORCEMENT

One of the most powerful management techniques you will ever use is differential reinforcement, which is defined as noticing and reinforcing positive behavior to reduce the negative. To use this technique, you must train yourself to look for what is right in your classroom and maximize the positive. Let this attitude become a way of life. Everywhere you go, everything you see will change when you develop the ability to see and appreciate the positive.

Most students want your approval and attention. Some need attention so desperately that they prefer negative attention to none. As strange as it seems, some students would rather be punished than ignored. Every behavior has its payoff. When students come to school with negative attitudes, they have learned to misbehave to call attention to themselves (an attempt to meet a need). The behavior may feel like a survival technique to them. You must discourage negative attention-getting behaviors as you seek to instill socially acceptable ways to fill needs. Consider the following examples of negative attention.

As you teach, John continues to interrupt. You might tend to:

- send him angry looks
- call his name angrily or write his name on the board
- punish him in some way

When you react in any of these ways, you reward John by paying attention to him. His negative bid for attention worked and he will use it again. Ask yourself, *What am I doing or not doing that contributes to John's behavior? How am I unconsciously giving John a payoff?* Keep in mind that you as well as John must change to solve the problem. As hard as it is to admit, you contribute to and even sustain John's behavior in some way.

Instead, control your tendency to send John negative messages. Look around and find students who are listening attentively. Sprinkle some of the following types of comments around the class.

"Jim and Bob are listening. I appreciate their courtesy and attention."

"A lot of students have their thinking caps on. I can feel their energy."

"Thank you for listening, Mary, Bob, Jim . . . "

Often, without a negative look or word from you, John will alter his behavior. Your encouragement of others also serves as a reminder to John, *Oh yes! I'm supposed to be . . .*

Be very quick to notice any positive change in John, as well as from the other children. John wants and needs your love. Tell John that you love him, believe in him, and know he can choose to make good choices. If you use proximity by moving closer to John, touching his desk, or touching him firmly, you assist him even more in redirecting his attention and behavior.

Any time you can accomplish your goals positively instead of negatively, you create an atmosphere of safety and support for your students. Not only will you help your students; you will like yourself better at the end of the school day. To assist you in integrating differential reinforcement, keep in mind that looking for what works brings much more contentment than constantly complaining about what is wrong.

Man becomes that which he gazes upon.

~George Harrison, Musician

BEHAVIOR MODIFICATION

Behavior Modification evolved from B.F. Skinner, as he carried out experiments reinforcing dogs. Because Skinner consistently fed dogs after ringing a bell, in time, the dogs salivated at the sound of the bell.

Unfortunately, you may discover students who are so lacking in motivation that you need an external reward to hook their attention. Two important questions for you to ask yourself include, *In what situations and with which children are concrete reinforcers appropriate, and how can behavior modification be used effectively and ethically?*

Advocates argue that life itself works on a system of reward and punishment. We remind ourselves, if you go to work, you get paid. Without the paycheck, you may not be willing to keep going to work. On the other hand, if you fail to show up, you may be removed from the payroll (which will feel like a punishment but is a natural consequence).

In an ideal world, teachers and parents rely on encouragement such as *thank you* and use consequences that fit the behavior such as *hitting others will get you removed from the game.* Unfortunately, not all children come from ideal situations. Some require more dramatic measures than encouragement and consequences.

A young but experienced teacher moved from an upper economic school to one surrounded by barbed wire, beer joints, and crack houses. To her dismay, the teacher discovered a total lack of interest in encouraging phrases, smiles, or acknowledgment of other children. Stickers and tokens meant nothing. Likewise, normal consequences and even punishment failed to make any difference.

The teacher had to ask herself, *What do angry children from gang-infested neighborhoods know and care about?* Children from violent situations deal with life at the survival and safety levels. The teacher decided to try non-sugar food treats and pennies to reward behavior. Due to the desperate level of need and the total lack of interest in learning, this teacher used drastic measures, which in a different learning environment would be inappropriate.

When a situation requires a behavior modification program, the following sequence serves as a guide for eventually weaning the students from extrinsic rewards to intrinsic feelings of satisfaction:

- Begin with concrete rewards accompanied by oral acknowledgment and encouraging body language. Initially, when teaching a new behavior, reward each time the desired behavior occurs. The younger the students, the more immediate the rewards must be.

- Gradually, lengthen the time between concrete rewards. Always provide oral and nonverbal reinforcement such as smiles whether you offer extrinsic rewards or not. Although you will no longer reward the behavior each time it occurs, you will continue to reward frequently.
- Space concrete rewards farther apart while maintaining all oral and nonverbal reinforcement.
- Call attention to the fact that participating in a certain way makes learning pleasant and helps students feel great.
- Set a long-term goal to gradually wean students from tokens to oral and nonverbal recognition.

Special Considerations

If your class needs a concrete reward system to get started, several considerations strengthen your efforts.

- Explain and model the desired behavior. Describe the behavior to be rewarded in specific and measurable terms; indicate what the behavior will look/sound like when it occurs, and what the quality will be. Rehearse the desired behavior.
- Be certain the students earn each reward. If you give a reward when behavior does not warrant one, you undermine your purpose—to establish and reinforce positive social behavior.
- If a warning or reminder is required, the behavior will not be rewarded. For example, Susie forgets her agreement to stay with her group and leaves during a brainstorming session. You give a nonverbal signal, and she returns. Susie does not earn a reward for staying with the group although you will thank her for making a good choice by returning.

- If students develop the annoying habit of insisting that you reward every positive act, say, "Sometimes I give stickers, and sometimes you get to simply feel good about yourself. I'll watch for you to repeat the behavior so you will get one next time."
- When you say, "I'm looking for students who have their books out, ready to learn," reward only the first students who get ready. Bobby, who takes 15 minutes to get his act together, will not be rewarded.

Unlike encouragers, rewards sometimes create envy in other students. If you have a child who needs a concrete reward system, you must decide whether to offer the same reward system to the entire class or to explain that Susie has special needs. **Fair doesn't mean everyone gets the same. Fair means everyone gets what is needed for learning success.**

If you design a special reinforcement program for Susie, make certain you orally and nonverbally notice the other children, or they will begin to copy Susie's inappropriate behavior to gain your attention.

Age Differences

When working with pre-kindergarten through second grade, focus on individual students. Whether using encouragement or concrete rewards, the younger students require more frequent attention and immediate gratification. Younger students focus on themselves more than on their peers. Notice the following examples of individual reinforcement.

- Susie, you must feel good about the way you finished early. Thank you (individual encouragement).
- John earned a marble toward extra free time (individual reward).

As students move from third grade into fourth and above, they become more peer-conscious. Being singled out may be embarrassing. Worse yet, the student who receives encouragement may be regarded as a teacher's pet and become a target for abuse and ridicule. With intermediate students, global encouragement and group rewards work more effectively than individual ones. Examples include:

- This class can feel good about . . . (group encouragement).
- The class earned another point toward a pizza party (group reward).

If you feel you must be more concrete to plant the seed of interest and motivation, concentrate on instilling enough dignity and self-worth that students will eventually become intrinsically motivated and rewarded. When students respond to internal motivation, they truly take responsibility for themselves. For all your students, keep saying, "I love this class. We are all learning together!" Students will live up or down to your expectations!

Final Thoughts on Behaviors

There are three possible reasons why a student misbehaves: she doesn't know better, she hurts, or she is chemically out of balance. Before a student can change behavior, she needs to express intense feelings in a socially acceptable way.

To assist your student in expressing feelings and emotions, hang circles with various facial expressions on yarn. When a student comes to class upset, she may choose a face that represents her feelings.

Sometimes students come from homes filled with arguing and putting one another down. They do not know that their behavior damages them socially. Explain to students, "I know you do _____ at home. Some behaviors that are fine at home are not acceptable at school." In some cases, you will need to provide specific examples of school behavior: "At school, we do not hit or kick others. We do not destroy books or papers. Curse words are not used at school."

The best actions in a good man's life are his little nameless, unremembered acts of kindness and love.

~William Wordsworth

ACTIVE LISTENING

Active listening, a communication tool developed by Thomas Gordon, serves the purpose of helping the listener become involved with the person sending the message. Use active listening when the other person feels upset and wants to communicate a problem to you. When you use active listening, your goals are to:

- Let the sender of the message know you are listening and understanding.
- Let the sender of the message know you care.
- Allow the sender to release some of the negative emotions.
- Encourage the sender of the message to solve the problem (with support from you).

Notice that the receiver of the message neither agrees nor argues with the sender. At the same time, active listening offers support and encourages additional communication. Active listening works with upset parents, principals, coworkers, and family members as well as children. To use active listening, you must be willing to:

- Listen to feelings that may be painful.
- Take time to stop and focus on the sender.
- Believe that the sender can solve his/her problems (with support).

When A Student Owns the Problem

When an upset student initiates the communication, the student owns the problem. Keep in mind that good communication is often made up of combinations of "I" messages and active listening. Below are some examples of student-owned problems.

- After an assignment is made, Bob begins crying and says the work is too long.

    Who owns the problem?

    Bob owns the problem. Bob is the one who is upset.

- Matthew tells you he feels stupid and plans to drop out of school after sixth grade.

    Who owns the problem?

    Matthew owns the problem because he is the one upset.

What if the student's message creates hurt, anxiety, or anger in you? How do you determine which needs must be addressed first? Consider the following example.

- Mary shouts that you are the worst teacher she has ever had.

  Who owns the problem?

  Mary owns the problem of being upset with you. You now own the problem of being hurt by Mary's remark.

Do you use active listening to help Mary or send an "I" message to help yourself? First, deal with Mary. Later, if you still feel a need, send the "I" message. As the adult in the situation, you have a responsibility to acknowledge Mary's feelings before your own.

Using Active Listening

Active listening includes a sequence. The first step is to give the sender feedback and check understanding.

- Feed the message back to reassure the student that you understand the message. You need to make certain you understand. There are ways to feed a message back: parroting, restating, or identifying the feeling behind the words.

  The easiest level is to simply parrot back the exact words that were said to you. "You just told me that you feel . . ."

  The second level is to say the same thing but in your own words. "Let me make certain I understand. You are saying that you . . . "(restate in your words).

> Perhaps the best feedback is a combination of, "What I heard you say was . . . " (wait for a response). "You seem to be feeling . . . " (wait for a response).

Restating the message in your own words has the benefit of checking your understanding of what you heard. The sender of the message will then confirm your understanding or clarify any confusion.

The second step in active listening is to use a door opener to encourage additional communication. You are assuring the sender that you are willing to listen.

> Door openers can be as simple as open body language, including leaning forward, uncrossing legs, and arms, and focusing on the student.

> Examples of other door openers include saying, "Tell me more. I have time to listen. And then. . .? OK. . ."

> Sometimes a door opener is a nod, a gesture, a pause. If you are sincere about wanting to listen, the sender will feel your intention.

•   After you have listened and given the sender enough time to fully express the feelings, move into the final step, which is to encourage the sender (even a young child) to problem-solve. Although you will help and guide, the problem belongs to the child. It is not yours to solve and, in most cases, you will not be able to fix the situation.

In summary, the three steps of active listening include: feeding back the message to check understanding, using door openers to encourage additional sharing, and encouraging personal problem-solving. Consider the following examples.

- Jim says, "Reading stinks!" Instead of either trying to convince Jim to like reading or shaming him for saying such a thing, use active listening:

Feedback	"You think reading stinks! You really seem to feel like a poor reader."
Door Opener	"Tell me about it."
Problem Solve	"What do you need in reading to feel more confident? What would help you like reading?"

- Ben says "I hate my dad." You happen to know Ben's dad is a good man. You want to scold Ben. Instead, you use active listening.

Feedback	"You are angry and upset."
Door Opener	"I understand. Keep talking."
Problem-Solve	"What could you do to feel better? What could your dad do? Can you suggest this to him?"

What About Abuse?

What must you do about a child in an abusive situation? How can that child be asked to solve the problem or to improve the situation caused by others? A child cannot control an addicted or abusive adult. However, even a young child can be encouraged to look for the antecedents (the behaviors that precede an outburst) and to be self-protective.

You can encourage responsible thinking and problem-solving by asking the following types of questions.

- "Even though you can't do anything about Dad's drinking, what can you do to protect yourself when he comes home drunk?"
- "How will you know your parent has been drinking too much? What behavior will send the signal that the situation is getting out of control?"
- "Where can you go? Whom can you call for help? Can you go to your room? Is there a place in your neighborhood that is safe?"
- "What can you say to yourself to stay calm? What do you need to remind yourself?"
- "What can I do to help?"
- "Do you have friends or relatives who can assist you?"
- "What would you like to see happen? What do you think would help your situation?"

If a child is neglected, abused, or molested, you are legally required to report suspicions. You do not have to observe the abuse firsthand, nor do you have to provide proof. Suspicion of abuse makes you legally responsible for reporting the situation to proper authorities. It is usually a good idea to confide in your school counselor and administrators before notifying your state's Department of Human Resources. Information can be given over the telephone, by fax, by e-mail, or in a letter. In making your report, you must be as objective and factual as possible. Document the time and day and exactly what the student shared with you.

Due to the fact that your student spoke in confidence, you will want to let the student know that you must seek assistance. Say, "I'm not trying to get your parents in trouble or hurt them. I care about them, and I believe they need help. Since you and I will not be able to solve the problem alone, we must ask others to join us in helping your family." You may be able to convince the student to go with you to share the confidence with your school counselor.

Your report will be kept anonymous to maintain your safety. The greater danger comes when the system becomes so overloaded that your student's case remains a low priority. This does not happen due to a lack of concern. The reality of most caseworkers is that they attend to infants, young children, and those whose lives appear to be in jeopardy before getting to older children. However, parents will be notified. In some cases, parents will increase the abuse as a warning to the child to never talk about the family situation again. Thus, there is always a fear of making bad matters worse.

As a teacher, you will agonize for the child and the family. Regardless of how swiftly or inadequately the authorities act in the situation, your most loving course of action will be to teach the child to watch for signs of danger and to do what the child can to protect herself and her siblings.

EMPOWERING TEACHERS

The greatest discovery of my generation is that human beings can alter their lives by altering their attitudes of mind.

~William James

NEUROLINGUISTIC PROGRAMMING

Wayne Dyer said, "If you change the way you look at things, the things you look at will change."

Seldom do any of us realize the subtle implications of color, music, movement, and slight-of-mouth suggestions and warnings that entice us to make daily decisions. Neurolinguistic Programming (NLP), a powerful communication tool that began in the 1970s, uses language to help people change their thoughts. After identifying the thought patterns of successful individuals, the founders began to teach these patterns to others. NLP, like many other powerful tools, shows up in courtrooms, political elections, and counseling sessions. It can be used constructively or negatively to manipulate others.

Used with honor, NLP offers a positive and powerful communication system for teachers. At a time when education needs both strong communication and impeccable integrity, few teachers know anything about NLP.

What is NLP?

NLP, the study of how the brain organizes, stores, and retrieves information regarding language and behavior, is the result of the combined thinking and research of John Grinder, Richard Bandler, and Leslie Cameron-Bandler. Working together, Bandler, Bandler, and Grinder integrated their knowledge of linguistics, psychology, and computer programming. Looking at the basic meaning of the terms offers clarity.

- *Neuro-* represents the nerves that consciously and unconsciously process thought throughout the brain and the body.
- *Linguistics* - refers to the words and language used to describe actual experiences.
- *Programming-* describes the internal pictures and messages, which make meaning of sensory information. For example, when you hear a siren, you probably conjure an internal picture of a fire truck. Likewise, seeing a fire truck makes it easy to imagine the sound of the siren.

Initially, the originators of NLP studied people with excellent communication skills. They determined that the strength of effective communication was not *what* was said but *how* it was said. By studying individuals with strengths in communication, they designed models and techniques that can be copied to achieve excellent communication.

Underlying Ideas are Called Presuppositions

The following ideas, called presuppositions in NLP, create a teaching tool for classroom and individual use.

Meaning of Communication Is the Response You Get

Have you ever explained something very clearly only to find your students in a state of confusion? Your reaction might be: "My communication skills are good. What's with those kids?" Oops! Your students' responses are telling you exactly what you communicated; not what you thought you said. In such a case, the appropriate response is, "Oh, I guess I didn't explain that quite the way I intended. Let me say it another way."

People Can Change

It is very easy to look at a student and think, *Hopeless. A dropout for sure!* Such an attitude does not consider the miraculous ability of the human spirit to rise above adversity and to change. Never give up.

On the last day of a five-day workshop, a fifteen-year-old girl visited a group of 140 teachers. The leader of the workshop asked the young lady to read aloud from the text being used in the workshop. All agreed that she read well. After the girl left, her foster mother, a teacher in the group, tearfully shared that the girl had lived with her for the past two years. Before that time, the young girl had been considered hopeless.

How many youngsters have we thrown away because change seemed impossible?

People Have All the Resources They Need

Within each student, there abides the ability to learn, to grow, to think, and to make wholesome decisions. If this seems impossible, it may help to realize that although we don't yet know how to tap into it, in our DNA we have the wisdom to grow a new arm. Your job, as a teacher, includes believing in each student and expecting each one to reach inside, with help, and find inner strengths and abilities. It is not yours to fix as much as an opportunity to encourage students to accept and believe in their personal ability and responsibility to succeed.

Flexibility Empowers Teachers and Students

If you only know one way to teach addition and it doesn't work, you will feel helpless and defeated. As you face your class day after day with the same strategy, both you and your students may feel like failures. Knowing many ways to teach a concept empowers you. If plan A doesn't work, try plans B, C, and D. By applying a variety of ideas, you reduce failure and frustration for your students as well as yourself.

Mental and emotional flexibility also empowers. For example, a teacher who was forced to transfer to a different school and grade decided that, although she could not change the situation, she could alter her attitude. She had one of her best years in a situation that looked like disaster.

Opposing Voices Do Not Mean You Are Crazy!

Have you ever wanted to go in two directions at once? For example, one part of your brain wanted to stick to your diet, but another part said, *Eat the cake. You deserve it!*

You may have an inner voice, often called a part, that says to write your lesson plans before watching television. Another voice responds, *You've had a hard day. Take a little time to relax. You know you already have the plan in your head. That's good enough.* As a teacher, you will experience a time when one part of you wants to give up on teaching and another part of you remembers how much you love the students.

Good news! You may be confused but not crazy. Everyone has these little parts and often the parts do not agree. Remember that each one seeks something good and pleasant for you. Say thank you to both (or all) inner voices for working so hard to take care of you. Determine what each one wants to accomplish for you. Ask the conflicting parts to work together for a solution that meets all needs.

If You Always Do What You've Always Done, You Will Always Get What You've Always Gotten

A depressed woman was once told, "If you don't like what you're getting in life, you need to make some drastic changes because the best predictor of the future is the past." Have you ever heard teachers say, "I've told those kids to sit down and be quiet 100 times today and they're still making too much noise." Perhaps it's long past time to do something different! One definition of insanity is doing the same thing over and over and expecting different results.

There Is No Failure — Only Feedback

Imagine the reduction of fear and anxiety when you realize that neither you nor your students will ever fail. You will get feedback that will indicate your next choice or direction. Based on feedback from the students, another teacher, your supervisor, or your reflections, you may choose to try a different approach. Changing does not imply failure but growth.

Likewise, your students will get feedback but will not fail in your classroom. Ideally, students will use feedback from you, their peers, parents, grades, and self-reflection to make needed changes. Some students will choose to disregard feedback and continue the same behavior. This does not mean the students are failing but only that additional feedback is required.

These students will continue to be disappointed until they get it. During times when students continue to ignore feedback and maintain what seems to be a losing position, you must remember that your role requires you to expect the best while providing feedback.

People Always Make the Best Possible Choice, Based on the Resources Available

No matter how unacceptable a behavior may be, it represents the best choice you or your students can make at that time, given the available emotions, understanding, and physical conditions. While this attitude eliminates judgment, hatred, and vengeance, it does not imply that you must accept unacceptable behaviors. We all do the best we can with what we've got, AND unacceptable behavior will not be accepted.

Yes, You Can Trust Your Unconscious

Your unconscious mind always learns and always seeks the best for you. If you hear an intuitive voice suggesting that you should do something, do it. Trust your intuition. Your unconscious mind learns many lessons that may not be consciously noticed and sends messages you would be wise to accept.

Students continue to learn, whether they realize it or not. Do you ever have a student fall asleep in class? Perhaps the unconscious mind gets all the facts needed. Even if the information does not go in, a student fighting to stay awake learns very little anyway. Why fight nature? How much do you learn when you find your eyes closing and your head nodding?

The Nature of the Universe Is Change

Some people demand change. Even if they teach the same grades and subjects year after year, they look for ways to make the experience different. Others find sameness more comfortable. Do you resent having to learn new skills or do you constantly seek innovative ideas? Do you fight technology? How do you feel about year-round schools? A preference for sameness or difference does not make you right or wrong.

However, change inevitably occurs. Nothing stays the same: not stones, icebergs, weather, or educational curriculum. Even if you want to keep things the same, take a deep breath and integrate the new into the old at a rate that fits your comfort level. Change equals growth. Change offers opportunity. Welcome it.

In his book titled, "Love," Leo Buscaglia says that if you don't believe in growth and change, you are in the process of dying. In a world that constantly bombards students with violence, sex, and the allure of wealth, schools must offer counter-attitudes. Can you, as a classroom teacher, offer the snap of MTV and video games? Probably not in your wildest dreams! However, below you will find some ways to use NLP to establish goals, bond learning with pleasure, and motivate students. Using the ideas as a background, consider the following suggestions from NLP.

Outcome Frames Equal Goals

An outcome frame is a goal that has been carefully examined in the areas of:

* benefits of the goal
* losses the goal could bring
* situations that block the goal
* resources needed to achieve the goal
* current and available resources

In addition, the goal is strengthened by imaging the visual outcome (how it will look), in auditory form (how it will sound), and kinesthetically (how it will feel). This scrutiny hopefully avoids creating a situation in which, "I want what I want until I get it!"

For example, a young lady desperately wanted a particular boyfriend until she hooked him. Then she lost interest. Another student applied for a scholarship, got it, and then decided against going to college.

Establishing a properly constructed goal will prevent some disappointments. The following steps will help you guide a student in the creation of a goal.

- Instead of mentally saying, *I do not want to fail,* say, *I want to make an A or B grade.*

- Ask the student, "How will you know if you get what you want? When will it occur? Where will you be? Who will be with you?" The student may say, "My friend Maddie and I will be in English together. When the papers are handed out, I will *see* my grade. I will *hear* Maggie congratulating me. I will *exchange high-fives with my friends.*

- Step three prevents the disappointment of reaching a goal and being surprised by unpleasant side effects by asking:
    - "What will you gain if you get this outcome?"
    - "What will you lose if you get this goal? Is there a reason not to have this outcome? Will you be hurt in any way?"
    - "Will the gains outweigh the things you stand to lose?"

A student wanted to read better but when asked if he had anything to lose by reading well, confessed that his mother wouldn't pay as much attention to him, and he wouldn't get to see his reading teacher whom he loved.

The student realized that along with the desired outcome would be some real or imagined losses. Looking at all possibilities allows the student to re-evaluate goals, to change or alter them, or to commit to wanting them 100%, which is what it takes to gain challenging outcomes.

- "Will anyone else gain or lose if you achieve your goal?" An outcome that benefits one will hopefully benefit all involved. This offers another opportunity to evaluate, reject, or claim the outcome.

- Step five will remind the student of personal responsibility for setting and achieving life dreams by asking, "What stops you?" This question puts the responsibility on the student.
- Ask, "What resources do you now have to help you gain this goal?" You hopefully will be a resource and support for the student.
- Finally, "What additional resources or help do you need to achieve what you want?"

Guiding a student through the development of a conceptualized goal offers the student motivation and direction. Not knowing what one wants, often results in achieving nothing. On the other hand, a student will avoid frustration and wasted time when she knows what the goal will look like, and sound like, and what the costs and rewards will be to obtain what she wants.

Breaking State Means Breaking a Bad Mood

A busy couple set aside an evening to stay home together and relax. During their conversation, a controversial topic came up and the mood instantly changed. One comment led to another in a downward spiral that threatened to ruin the evening. Suddenly one said, "This conversation isn't going anywhere but down. Let's break out of this bad mood." At that point, both changed their body positions from slouched to upright, frowns to more pleasant facial expressions, and they moved to another room. When stuck in an unproductive, negative pattern, making physical changes will help break a bad mood.

Consider the following classroom example of breaking a bad mood. After three rainy days, a teacher and his class felt grumpy and moody. Students grumbled about assignments and refused to listen to one another or the lesson. The teacher realized that continuing to do the same activity could only result in sinking lower and lower into class depression and resistance.

Wisely, the teacher stopped the class mid-lesson and said, "Put your books away and we'll change what we are doing. " As students cleared their desks, the teacher put on some lively music and changed his negative body language by smiling, straightening up, and moving purposefully. He then brought the students to the carpet for a meaningful discussion on a different topic. The physical changes broke the negative state of mind for the class as well as for the teacher.

When you or your students feel angry, bored, or resistant, you quickly realize how unproductive and unresourceful the state of mind can be. When in a negative place, you usually find it difficult, if not impossible, to recall and make use of your resources and strengths. A negative mood is not likely to change without a total shift in mind and body. Although it may be important to return to a critical issue later, you will experience more gains by getting yourself and your students in a more positive frame of mind.

Break negative patterns in safe and respectful ways. The following examples offer appropriate ways to break moods in a classroom.

- Use music to increase energy, change the atmosphere, or calm feelings.
- Change body and facial expressions.
- Tell a joke or appropriate story.
- Use physical stretching as an activity to break a pattern.
- Ask students to get up and change seats every 20 to 30 minutes to interrupt boredom, avoid lethargy, and keep circulation moving.
- During class, ask students to stand for one to three minutes and continue the lesson from a standing position. Standing gives a different perspective.
- From time to time, let the students applaud for themselves. Clapping stimulates additional circulation and improves attitude.

- Touching a student lightly on the shoulder can break a negative state. Eye contact can also be a very important way to stop a problem before it gains momentum.
- Ask the whole class to take a slow, deep breath to break out of a negative feeling.
- Use props such as hats, bells, and masks to change the mood in the classroom.
- Experience nature by caring for pets, planting a garden, or taking guided walks as wonderful ways to break a negative mood.

Using the Senses

Senses or "submodalities" are visual scenes and sounds recorded mentally and emotionally. For example, feelings of fear and inhibition get in the way of learning and amount to unproductive, unresourceful behavior. Often, a talented and intelligent student holds back because of fear (thus failing to use the resources of talent or intellect). It is possible that the student's fear is not based on reality but on sensory memories. You desperately want to guide the student to a positive attitude. Consider the following story for ideas.

A talented athlete gets in a slump. Usually, she bats well but, in her slump, she strikes out or fails to get on base. First, help her determine the goal that she desires (see Outcome Frame or Goals above on page 61). Ask her to relax, close her eyes, and get a mental picture of herself getting a strong, solid hit.

Once the athlete creates an inner picture, encourage her to make the picture brighter, add color, make it larger, and add the sound of fans cheering. Ask the student to step into the picture and to associate (that is, feel) the power of the hit, and the pleasure of running the bases. Tell her to live the experience in the first person.

As you suggest each idea, watch the student carefully. The better the image, the more relaxed and deeper the breathing will be. If the student's breathing becomes shallow or if she holds her breath, go a different direction. In NLP terms, this is called calibrating the student, meaning paying close attention. (Most people do this unconsciously when they talk to people.)

For example, when you suggest adding color, if the student becomes stressed instead of excited, cease visual suggestions. However, if imagining the sound of cheering fans produces a positive expression, relaxed posture, and deeper breath, add a band, and whistles to the image.

Ways to change the **visual** picture (referred to as the visual submodality) include the following ideas:

- Vary the intensity of color from black and white to very bright colors.
- Change the distance from far away to close and personal.
- Alter depth perception by going from a flat to a three-dimensional image.
- Add clarity by going from a blurred to a clear picture.
- Create a boundary by putting the picture within a picture frame.
- Expand the picture to a panoramic view that continues around behind the individual.
- Add movement by changing from a still photo to a movie.

Ways to alter the **auditory** sense impressions include:

- Vary the pitch of the sound from high-pitched screaming to a low roar.
- Change the volume from louder to softer.
- Alter the rhythm by adding chanting or rapping.
- Add music or other appropriate sounds.
- Create internal dialogue.

The **kinesthetic** sensation can create changes in the student's imagery by changing the:

- movements in the picture
- location of people or places
- attitudes and feelings
- temperature
- texture

Before asking the student to open her eyes, suggest that in the future, if she feels anxious, she can recall and re-experience the visualization she created. Encourage her to recall the images as often as possible. You have given your student a tool for accessing a positive mood regardless of the outer situation. You have also taught her to use her submodalities - visual, auditory, and tactile/kinesthetic, in an internal visualization.

Act As-If (Focus on Your Goal)

After your student thinks through and creates a strong goal, help her secure the idea for future use by taking an *as-if* attitude. Lead your student through the following steps to help her bring the goal into reality.

- Imagine that it is six months from now.
- Imagine you've made many changes over the last six months. Which change is most pleasing to you?
- What did you do to make changes?
- Act as if you already have achieved your goal.

Future Pace to Strengthen Recall

An activity that is like As-If is referred to as a Future Pace. Use the following activity to help forgetful students recall something that needs to be done in the future, such as getting notes signed. Ask the student to establish a sequence of reminders using three different modalities (senses) to help remember to get a parent's signature.

- See the specific room, furniture, and place to get the note signed. Notice who is present (visual).
- Determine a sound that will be occurring as the note is signed (auditory).
- Imagine an activity that will serve as a cue to getting the note signed (kinesthetic).

A student may think, I'll hear the click of the lock as I see my mom walk in the door. As she sets her bag on the table, I'll show her the note from school and ask her to read and sign it. The sound of the lock and the sight of Mom will be my reminders.

Reframing Thinking

When a student gets stuck with a negative attitude, you can create a new interpretation of the event. There are two different ways to change (reframe) her thinking. One method keeps the same event but thinks of a different interpretation. This is called a *content reframe*. Your purpose is to encourage the student to think differently about herself. Examples of content reframes include:

Undesired Behavior	Content Reframe
Hyperactivity in class	"I love your energy. You must be ready to learn!"
Watching too much TV	"Some people learn from television by choosing programs that teach them new ideas."
Talking in class	"You have so many great ideas."

Failing math	"Your grades are giving me information about your strengths and needs. Now I will know how to help you."
Hitting and fighting	"You are really trying to take care of yourself. This is good. Although I want you to take care of yourself, I can show you some other ways to protect yourself."

Another way to reframe is to accept the behavior but suggest using it at a more appropriate time and place. In a different context, the behavior may be beneficial. This is called a *context reframe*. The following examples demonstrate ways to reframe the behaviors above.

Undesired Behavior	Context Reframe
Hyperactivity in class	"I love your energy. All that activity will be great for our baseball team. Save it for the game!"
Watching too much TV	"Watching television is a great rainy-day activity. You can enjoy the outdoors on sunny days."
Talking in class	"You do such a good job talking. You will be a great reporter for your group when the time comes."
Failing math tests	"Because of your own difficulties, you will always be very kind and understanding when helping younger children."
Hitting and fighting	"There was a time when this behavior helped you take care of yourself. You are safe here and you do not need to protect yourself by hurting others."

Circle of Excellence

Circle of Excellence, a tool that establishes positive feelings, strengths, and confidence, helps prepare for challenging events. Research indicates that the subconscious mind cannot tell the difference between a rehearsal of an event and the event itself. This means that you can mentally practice an event using the best resources available. When the actual situation occurs, resources such as self-confidence and enthusiasm will be in place.

One teacher used this activity to help prepare for a presentation at a national conference. Being rather shy, the teacher initially faced the presentation with extreme anxiety. With guidance, she recalled times when she had been very confident, happy, and successful. In her imagination, she reviewed earlier successful feelings and practiced bringing these past resources (positive feelings) to the conference presentation. Because the teacher knew her material and was fully capable of speaking, the extra boost of confidence helped her relax and even enjoy delivering her lecture.

In a different situation, a physical education major had trouble with behavior management during her student teaching experience. She was encouraged to recall times when she felt like a winner on her softball team. The student teacher was able to remember and re-experience feeling in charge, respected, and powerful. After bringing these feelings of confidence (her resources) to the classroom, her methods of dealing with students' behaviors changed and she became known for her fair, yet firm behavior management system. The important difference was a result of an internal shift. She felt differently about herself and, therefore, made the needed external changes with her students.

Although Circle of Excellence does not develop knowledge or competence when these qualities are missing, the activity becomes a powerful way to enhance skills and abilities when self-esteem is faltering. To help yourself or a student add confidence to competence, use the following steps.

- Imagine a circle on the floor or a beam of light coming from the ceiling. Make the circle or beam a favorite color.
- Stand outside the imagined circle. Recall a time when you felt strong, powerful, confident, and happy. (If recalling such a time seems impossible, imagine someone else having a powerful experience).
- Step into the circle and experience the feelings of the previous success. Feel yourself (or the imagined person) bursting with confidence and happiness.
- Step outside the circle. Repeat stepping into the circle and recreating the powerful feelings until the feelings come easily.
- Step outside the circle. Think of a future time when these powerful feelings of success will be good resources for you. Quickly step into the circle and link the past feelings with the future event.

We can let go of the past and the future. Now is the only time you have, and each instant is for giving.

~Principles of Attitudinal Healing

COMMUNICATION EMPOWERMENT

Not only can NLP help students, but it also submits powerful teaching tools for increasing effectiveness in the classroom. Keep in mind that you continually influence your students. By being aware of the effects of your actions, expressions, and words, you can influence positively and avoid inadvertently creating a negative connection.

Power Stance

When wanting to get your students' attention, your actions say more than your words. Apply the following nonverbal communication.

- Move to the front center of the room.
- Stand very still with your weight evenly distributed and your feet aligned with your shoulders.
- Hold your hands together in front or behind you.
- Deliver a brief message.
- For added clarity, write page numbers and directions on the chalkboard.
- If you move, students will move also. If your weight tilts off center, what you say lacks certainty. As soon as you get centered (mentally focused, spiritually aware, and physically balanced) you create a teaching position that communicates both love and purpose.

Giving Directions

When you say, "Take out your math books and turn to page 40," what happens? As soon as students hear the words "Take out _____," they immediately begin scrambling for math books and fail to hear the page number. You will then hear a chorus of, "What page?" Two ways to avoid this confusion include the following ideas.

- Say, "On page 40, you will be doing 1 through 20." Write the message on the board. Now, get out your math books. You saved the message to get out math books until the end.
- An even better option is to use a traffic cop's signal and say, "In a minute you will be getting out your math books. You will do 1 through 20 on page 40." Remove the cop's stop signal as you say, "Get out your books."
- Always write directions on the chalkboard as well as stating them.

Writing Directions on the Board

If possible, write your directions on the chalkboard before students arrive. This frees you to welcome students and to get the class off to a good start. However, in some situations, you will find it impossible to get your board work done before the students come to class.

If you get the attention of the class and ask them to wait while you write directions on the board, the students will not wait quietly when you turn your back to write. This means, at the end of your writing task, you must establish attention once again. By getting attention and then losing it during the time it takes to write on the board, you anchor the message, *It isn't important to pay attention. Nothing is happening anyway.*

If you must write on the board while students wait, consider two ways to accomplish this.

- Let students talk quietly among themselves as you write. As soon as you finish, give a signal, get their undivided attention, and explain the directions.
- State the assignment, let the ones who rely on auditory input get started, and assure the rest that you will write directions and page numbers on the board.

Most Important Twenty Seconds

Once you have taught a lesson and assigned independent work, you will instruct students to begin. At that time—as students begin the assignment—model a tone of quiet and concentration by freezing for 20 seconds.

As you wait for 20 seconds, scan the room looking for signs of confusion or inattention. Once you have spotted your problems and indicated with a hand signal that you will be with them, slowly and quietly move to redirect and answer questions.

Use Nonverbal Signals

Talk less and act more. You may have heard the saying, "What you do speaks so loudly, I can't hear what you say." This is especially true for kinesthetic students who often do not notice auditory signals but respond to your body messages. Let your goal be to communicate more by saying less.

In terms of managing students' behavior, the more you can communicate without speaking, the stronger your message will be. If you say, "Sit still and listen to directions," as you scurry around the room passing out papers, your students process your nonverbal message and continue talking and moving. As soon as you get still, centered, and quiet, your message will be received. You may not even need to state the request for attention.

Often in classes, the same student's name gets called out negatively time and again. When this occurs, the student gets some type of secondary gain (i.e., attention or control). Another disadvantage of using oral communication to correct the student is that you add to the noise level in the classroom. The common practice of saying *shh* adds irritation as well as additional noise and almost always fails to impact students.

One study indicated that nonverbal communication is 82% more powerful than your oral message. Examples of nonverbal messages include:

- looking directly at students while waiting for attention
- giving a coach's time-out signal
- motioning for students to sit
- using a music conductor's motion for quiet
- acting out a traffic cop's signal to stop

- pointing to a paper or book
- giving a thumbs up/down signal
- using sign language for yes/no
- winking, frowning, smiling
- giving a silent cheer
- pausing mid-sentence and letting the sentence hang as you wait for students' attention

Sometimes, if it fits your personality, be outrageous. When students were getting too noisy, one teacher opened her umbrella and sat down. After all the students were quiet, she said, "I thought there was a storm brewing; there was so much thunder in here."

Physically Model Behavior You Want

A rule frequently seen in classrooms is, "Raise your hand before speaking." It seems like a good idea but what about the times you want students to be excited and spontaneous? What about the times when a choral response seems more productive than raising hands?

A better idea encourages students to create a rule about respecting one another with the agreement that when you want hands to be raised, you will signal by raising your own. When you want answers from anyone and everyone, you will use another hand signal, such as open, or receiving hands.

Initially when teaching students to notice and respond to signals, you will orally state exactly what you want as you physically indicate the desired behavior. Be certain to link the two together until the words are anchored to the nonverbal signal.

- Raise your hand just before phrasing a question.
- Say, "I want everyone to think about this question and raise your hand if you know . . ."
- Ask the question, pause, and call on a student whose hand is raised.

You have given both an oral and a nonverbal message. Eventually, after students understand your signal, you will no longer need the oral reminder and you can obtain the desired behavior using only the signal.

Be Congruent When Communicating

Whether you feel happy or upset, make certain your face, body, and voice convey the same message. For example, if you smile as you say, Stop, the students will believe the smile and ignore the oral message.

A school librarian recently told a class, "You did a good job in the library today." As she spoke to the class, she frowned and stood with her arms crossed. Was she congruent? What message did the students get? The class did not appear to feel complimented.

What about the teacher who said to a student, "I really believe you can learn to do algebra," as he shook his head no and looked away. Why did the student leave feeling, "He did not mean what he said to me?"

Avoid Double Messages

The way you state your message makes a difference in the way your students respond. If you say, "Don't run," your students hear the *run* and ignore or fail to process the *don't*. Nine times out of ten, they run immediately after you have told them not to do so!

- Instead of saying, "Don't run," phrase your message, "Walk slowly."
- Instead of saying, "Don't talk." – "Work quietly."
- Instead of saying, "Don't be rude." – "Be courteous."

If you forget and send a double message, correct it immediately by following these steps:

- Breathe deeply.
- Step to one side.
- Change your voice volume.
- Say, "What I meant to say was . . ."

Match, Break, Lead

Occasionally, especially during cooperative learning, the noise level in a classroom becomes awesome. If you need to match the noise (to be heard), you may speak more loudly to break the state of confusion and lead the class to a calmer climate.

- If the class has trouble hearing and seeing you, use a clap, a bell, a bicycle horn, or some attention-getting music to <u>match</u> the noise in the room.
- Pause. Remember that a pause can be your most important nonverbal signal. The pause breaks the state of noise and confusion and opens the opportunity to lead students to a calmer, quieter state. During the pause, you must remain quiet and still.
- Following a brief pause, speak in a voice barely above a whisper. By dropping the volume of your voice, you <u>lead</u> the students to a quieter noise level in the classroom.

Noisy teachers usually have loud, boisterous classrooms. Quiet, firm teachers usually have quiet classes. If you match the noise level but fail to pause or to speak in a soft voice you sabotage your desire for a quieter classroom.

Communicating with Polarizers

Some students tend to *polarize*—or take the opposite position—from any teacher or adult in authority. Usually, the student who constantly argues has not successfully gained a personal identity. In NLP terminology, the student has not individuated. This student instinctively and subconsciously desires personal identity. Taking the opposite position on an issue, implies, *I am me. I have an opinion of my own.*

When working with a student who tends to argue (regardless of the point of view), you will discover that telling or even suggesting, what the student should do invites a reverse reaction. Often, a story with a subtle message gets a much more positive effect. (See section on Metaphors on page 94.)

Arguing with a student who wants to take the opposite position creates futility and frustration. One reason the situation remains hopeless is that if you agree with the student, she will flip opinions. Ways to respond to a student who polarizes include using the following statements.

- "I can see why you said that. It's an interesting way to look at this issue."
- "Some people believe . . ."
- "There's some truth in your thinking."
- "Thank you for bringing up that question. It helps us grow to look at all sides of an issue."
- "It's OK for us to think differently. Divergence makes life interesting."
- "That's a challenging question. I appreciate your bringing it up."

In truth, your polarizer will help you grow if you remember your sense of humor and don't take the opposition personally.

Check it Out By Calibrating

To *calibrate* means to check out, to make certain. Calibrating goes beyond reading body and facial language to interpreting more subtle clues. For example, while you explain a point, a student at the front of the room frowns. If you have not previously noticed and categorized the student's various expressions, you read the frown as a look of confusion or disagreement. In truth, the student understands perfectly, and the frown indicates her agreement with a powerful and poignant idea. If you misinterpret and continue to explain, the student will become bored.

Begin calibrating students by noticing each student's body language, facial clues, oral expressions, eye patterns, and signals of pleasure and stress. If uncertain about what a student feels, ask. Once you mentally collect information about each student, you will be able to accurately read levels of interest, fatigue, and excitement, as well as levels of understanding.

Effective teachers intuitively notice and interpret the subtle communication of their students. Some teachers seem to be born with the art of calibrating and understanding their students. They adeptly make needed adjustments to enhance growth and learning. Even these teachers can improve. Others, lacking an instinct, can learn the science of calibrating. To strengthen the ability to calibrate, be aware of, and respond to the following types of indicators:

- shifts in body weight, a tilt of the head, or movement of arms and legs
- tapping fingers, crossing, or uncrossing legs, clenching fists
- changes in skin color, flared nostrils, lower lip movements, and changes in the muscles around the eyes

- voice changes in rate, tone, hesitations, and word emphasis
- the rise and fall of the shoulders and chest

Breathing may be high in the chest or lower towards the abdomen, shallow to deep, slow, or fast. Usually, high shallow breathing indicates stress.

Several years ago, a less resourceful student teacher wondered why she wasn't successful with her class of first graders. After all, she did everything just the way the book advised. What could be the problem? Careful observation revealed that the teacher paid no attention to the wiggles and whispers of the first graders. Long after they tired, her lessons droned on endlessly. Looks of confusion were disregarded. Since she seemed unable or unwilling to read (calibrate) frustration, boredom, and intimidation, her behavior and attitude toward the children remained inappropriate.

Be aware that students always seek to communicate with you. As you get to know your students, you learn to interpret what the various communication patterns mean.

Whole Class Calibration

To calibrate your class visually, create a mental picture during a time when the students demonstrate interest, motivation, and excitement. Scan the room and create a visual memory of their faces and body positions.

During a time when the students demonstrate a lack of interest, repeat the exercise. In your visual memory, record pictures of the way the students look individually and as a whole class. Notice the contrasts and watch for changes.

Using auditory processing, do the same activity. At a time when learning is taking place, notice the sounds in the classroom. There may be a soft hum of appropriate mumble reading or the shared whispers of learning groups.

You may hear occasional laughter. Although not hospital quiet, the hum of productive learning fills the classroom.

Contrast the sounds of a room out of control. Raucous laughter, loud voices, and inappropriate comments assault you. Chairs scrape, the pencil sharpener grinds, and children argue. When the noise level and the sounds feel unpleasant to you, students cannot learn.

Body language provides your clue to kinesthetic calibration. Small groups that sit close, lean forward, look at one another, and smile, are different from groups that sit apart, turn their backs on one another, cross their arms, frown, and constantly look for reasons to walk away.

If you spend your days putting out endless brush fires, calibrate your class for boredom, confusion, frustration, or excitement and make immediate changes. If the lesson isn't working, it will not get better until you break the negative state in your classroom. (See Breaking State Means Breaking a Bad Mood on page 63.)

Individual Calibration

You can calibrate individual students as well as whole classes. When working with an individual student, notice facial expression, voice tone, breath flow, and body language as the student experiences various emotions. If you make a mental note of the changes in advance, you will have a reference point when observing the student during learning situations. To establish these references, spend some time getting to know the student.

- Ask the student a question that you know will create confusion. Calibrate the appearance, sounds, and movements of the student. Store the memory so you will always recognize confusion in this student.
- Elicit happiness and excitement in the student. Again, calibrate for future reference.

Once you can recognize various emotions in each of your students, you will be able to gauge understanding, confusion, insecurity, and excitement throughout the day. As needed, you can adjust.

Calibrating Incongruence

Watch for incongruence. When words do not match body language, read the nonverbal signals. For example, a student may say, "Yes, I understand," while crossing arms, frowning, or looking down.

Another example of incongruence includes the student who says, "I don't know anything about this graffiti," while avoiding your eyes, flushing slightly, and shifting weight. Chances are the student knows a lot about this graffiti.

Still, another example of incongruence involves the parent who assures you, "We'll find time to help Jane with her homework," as the parent's shoulders seem to sag with the weight of a new burden, the face seems to be saddened, and eyes and mouth frown. The parent probably wants to help but if you calibrate the nonverbal communication, you know you cannot count on home support.

Gaining Rapport

If someone says, "That teacher has a good rapport with his students," the person means that the teacher communicates well, understands students, and students feel safe with the teacher. For some teachers, this comfortable and necessary bonding comes easily. Usually, a teacher who gains rapport with students shows personal interest in students and unconsciously does one or more of the following:

- matches the student's body language
- matches the student's words
- matches the student's facial expression

Gaining rapport through matching, sometimes called mirroring, can be learned. Mirroring sends the message that says, *I am willing to look at life through your view (your map of reality)*. Teachers with integrity use mirroring to gain rapport and to assist students. Consider the following stories of individual and group rapport.

Middle School Boy Example

A young middle school student was referred for testing and remediation. The student was twelve, Hispanic, a member of a gang, and reading at a second-grade level. School had not been a happy experience for him and the last thing he wanted to do was talk about his reading problem with another teacher.

At first, the teacher greeted him warmly and began chatting in a friendly voice and open body language. To every question, the student's reply was, "I don't know" or "I don't care," delivered with his head down, body slouched, and arms crossed.

Suddenly, the teacher realized, *I am out of rapport with him. He is trying to communicate his anger and discouragement and I am acting like a cheerful Mary Poppins*. With that realization, the teacher matched the student's slouch, lowered her tone of voice, slowed her speech, crossed her arms, and asked, "You are miserable at school, aren't you?"

Recognizing and matching the student's message created the space for honesty. Gradually, he shared some of his school experiences, his disappointments, and his meager and fragile hopes. As the student relaxed, the teacher slowly changed to more open and friendly mannerisms.

Gradually, the student followed. At the end of the session, the student stood and hugged the teacher. He had been understood.

Gaining group rapport will assist you with classroom management challenges.

Student Teaching Example

The following story comes from an experience in physical education.

A first-year physical education teacher in a low-income school was upset by the rude way her students talked to one another. Corrections were largely ignored until she gained rapport by saying, "No one in my class gets to diss me. No one gets to diss other students in this class." The inner-city students understood and responded to the communication when it came in their language. Gaining rapport is as critical with older students and adults as it is with children.

Remedial Teacher Example

The teacher in the story below reversed a negative attitude early in the year. A teacher was hired to teach remedial reading to freshmen. Not only did the teenagers hate reading because of their negative anchors, but they were also insulted by having to take this required reading course. On the first day of class, most of the students slunk into the classroom with scowling faces. It was not difficult for the teacher to calibrate their level of unhappiness.

Realizing that the students were upset and resistant, the teacher gave them ample opportunity to tell her how unfair it was to have to take her class. She was careful to listen without becoming defensive. She was also careful to avoid either agreeing or disagreeing.

Eventually, she asked the students to write letters describing their feelings, read the letters to one another, and then tear the letters into small pieces. She concluded by stating, "I understand how you feel. However, we are going to be together for a full semester. You can choose to be angry every day or you can choose to make the best of a situation. It's up to you."

By calibrating the students and realizing their need to express themselves, she helped them release their negative energy. All but one chose to cooperate for the rest of the semester.

When Open Body and Positive Expressions Fail

Teachers have been taught that individuals with good communication skills open their arms, uncross their legs, smile, give eye contact, lean forward, and talk cheerfully. Usually, these mannerisms work appropriately and gain positive results. However, when faced with an angry or discouraged student, you may need to initially alter these practices until you gain the trust of the student. Only after gaining rapport will you begin to gradually lead the student to more positive communication.

To communicate with an angry student, you will need to begin by mirroring the student. You gain rapport if you match the crossed arms, the harsh voice, and the frowning face and say, "You're upset!" Listen and observe. Calibrate your student. As the student begins to drop defensiveness and become more trusting, lead her to a more relaxed, positive body language by gradually changing your own.

Please make note of the following two cautions. First, mirror out of respect rather than to trick or manipulate. When in France, act like the French have a respectful attitude. It is courteous to match a student if you intend to put the student at ease. Second, you must be subtle. Miming belittles a student. Your gestures, movements, and facial expressions must be gradual and as natural as possible.

MOTIVATION

I am only ten and I love this book. Amazingly, I love this book. I used not to read, but now I read, read, and read.

~Bryan O., 4th Grade

MOTIVATION IN THE CLASSROOM

What teacher doesn't want to know how to motivate students? Some students need to be motivated to begin a task. Others begin but have trouble completing assignments. Systems of punishments and rewards work minimally and only with some students. The following list of motivators represents tried-but-true ideas for motivating students.

- Dignify all wrong answers by showing why a student's answer seems plausible while giving the student the correct information. See page 102.

- Demonstrate ways the skills and knowledge learned at school relate to the real world.

- Show how information, skills, and knowledge immediately improve students' lives.
- Offer a variety of instructional formats. For example, sometimes use cooperative learning, sometimes use whole group discussion, and sometimes hold individual conferences.
- Change your voice tone and body language. Sometimes make your voice mysterious, excited, slow, and deliberate, or sometimes speak barely above a whisper.
- If you see students getting unmotivated and bored, increase the pace of your lesson.
- End passive listening and integrate physical activity. Stop what you are doing and implement a hands-on activity.
- Invite students to stand up for a few minutes as you continue the lesson.
- Ask each student to change places with someone across the room to gain a new perspective.
- If your students seem overwhelmed, slow the pace of your lesson. You may need to reteach using a different strategy or sensory modality.
- Unmotivated students can be jarred out of boredom with a quick, low-stress activity using competition.
- Encourage motivation by saying, "It's OK not to know. It's not OK not to think. Think about this question before raising your hand."
- Not knowing who will be called on motivates some students. Sometimes say, "Put your hands down. I have a list in my head, and I know which students I plan to call on."

Most students will respond to the suggestions above. However, some students have specific areas where motivation breaks down.

Motivating to Start a Task

Some students feel overwhelmed by an assignment because they believe the effort required will be too great. They may not believe they can achieve success. Consistent encouragement offers one way to motivate students to begin. In addition, teach students to use self-talk along with visualization.

- Encourage the student to say, "It will be great to get started on this report!"
- Instruct students to accompany self-talk with an internal picture of the finished project, a big smile, and a good feeling.
- Teach the student to say, "All right, I'll do it."
- The student begins the task.
- Have the student say, "It is fun to begin something new and different!"
- Instruct the student to say, "I see myself getting all the tools, information, and materials together. I see myself starting.

Motivating to Finish a Task

The motivation strategy above works well except for students who tend to visualize the finished project so thoroughly that they sometimes convince themselves it is already done. These students have no difficulty seeing, experiencing, and enjoying the big picture, but often fail to complete the small steps to reach the result. Teach your right brain, global student the following self-talk and visualization.

- Encourage the student to mentally notice, *I see that the job is not complete. The page is blank. The report is not yet written.*
- Encourage the student to do one step (even if it isn't the logical first step). The goal is to get started and progress from there!
- After each ste, the student must notice that the project is not finished and tackle another step (although not necessarily the next logical step).

Toward or Away from Motivation

In methodology courses, pre-service teachers usually learn to motivate students in positive ways rather than with threats of punishment. The positive should work and usually does. Those students who respond to positive reinforcement are students who find moving toward something rewarding and exciting. NLP refers to this as a *toward-motivation- strategy.*

Other students do not seem to respond to positive reinforcement. Your principal or supervisor may suggest, "Perhaps if you offer additional tangible rewards the student will care enough to do the work. Maybe you should be more frequent and consistent with the positive reinforcement." If you try these suggestions and the problem persists, you may be dealing with a student who has an *away-from-motivation strategy.*

Although you always prefer to motivate positively, there will be a few students whose motivation comes from avoiding unpleasant consequences. For these students, offer choices such as, "You may do your work now or during free time. You decide." If the student perceives losing free time as a negative, the student will be motivated to move away from this possibility.

Sameness or Difference Motivation

Some students need and want situations to remain the same. They are more easily motivated when their environment remains stable with an observed schedule.

Other students crave differences. These students thrive on a variety of teaching/learning strategies and conditions. If you teach math differently each day, these students will be motivated and interested. Asking students to do the same lessons in the same manner day after day kills motivation for the students who prefer differences.

How do you meet the needs of both kinds of learners? Be aware that your routines and schedule need to stay the same to satisfy the needs of your *sameness* students. Within each lesson, you will meet the needs of your students who want differences by offering a variety of strategies and ways to learn. If you keep the same daily schedule and consistently teach new concepts a minimum of three different ways, you will meet the needs of both types.

Offer choices to all students such as, "You may choose to work your math problems using manipulatives, using your fingers, or on the computer."

Another example of choice suggests, "You may choose to stay at your same desk to do the work, move to the learning center, the private office area, or the standing desks." Students who prefer to keep the situation the same will usually stay at their desks. Students who prefer differences often use a new option every day.

METAPHORS TO MOTIVATE

In English, you learn that similes compare two unlike items using the words like or as. English metaphors compare unlike things without using the words, like or as. Both provide powerful mental images. In NLP, metaphors amount to either personal experiences or make-believe tales told for a purpose. Some metaphors use succinct statements, while others engage in lengthy stories.

If the metaphor is subtle, the communication to the unconscious mind is stronger. Speaking to the unconscious mind has the advantage of getting around all the resistance and arguments of the conscious mind. Metaphors work well with the student who polarizes and resists everything you suggest.

An example of a metaphor used with a young girl who had not emotionally separated from her mother (thus had not individuated or formed her own identity) is paraphrased in the following story.

A beautiful plum tree grew on the side of a hill. As spring came, the twigs of the plum tree began to swell with buds and in time, the buds grew to blossoms. Then gradually the blossoms began to fade and fall to earth. Behind them began the deep red fruits of the plums.

Each day the plums grew. Soon the plums became ripe. Birds came and ate the plums. Sometimes, the birds dropped plums to the ground.

One of the plums that fell to the ground wrinkled and dried and left a small seed. The grasses covered the seed, and the seed found itself deep in the earth. Soon it began to put out its roots and seek nourishment.

As the roots grew, a new little plum tree began to grow and by the end of winter, the little tree looked like a small twig. In time, the young plum tree gathered its strength so that when spring came, it too put forth blossoms and fruit, separate from the parent tree nearby.

End the story here. Avoid making a comparison or drawing a conclusion. If you use the metaphor well, the student hears the message and decides to emotionally separate from her mother without ever realizing you had any input.

A review of Aesop's fables will give you a collection of stories that contain good metaphors. For example, in *The Hare and the Tortoise,* the rabbit, who runs very fast gets beaten by the slow, plodding tortoise because the tortoise persists and stays with the task until the end. In another example, *The Shepherd Boy and the Wolf,* the boy repeatedly fools people by calling for help when he doesn't need it. When the time comes that he needs assistance, no one comes.

Same Words - Different Context

Quick, simple statements often offer the most powerful metaphors. When working with an individual student, use the student's words or meaning in a different context if possible. Notice the use of hard work in a different context.

- A student says, "Math is hard work." You nod and reply, "Have you ever watched ants getting ready for winter? Some carry pieces of food or leaves bigger than their bodies. It's hard work (repeat the child's words) to carry a load that large. I imagine they'll be happy when winter comes, and they will be warm and well-fed. All that hard work will pay off in the future."

You may not need to use the exact words, only the message of the student's comment. Notice implied confusion in the metaphor below which reflects the student's feelings.

- A student says, "I can't make a decision." You might say, "I once knew a young girl who wanted to change her life but couldn't decide on anything. One day she said to herself, 'Just decide to do something. If it's not right, you can change your mind later.' Even though she took a class she didn't need, the decision to act got her back in school and got her started on a new path."
- A student struggling to form letters was asked, "What skill seems easy for you?" When the boy shared his ability to draw, the teacher replied, "Drawing and writing require some of the same skills. If you can draw well, you can use the same abilities to form letters."

Objects create good metaphors. What type of individual might benefit from the following metaphor about tree twigs?

- *A dry and brittle twig will break when bent. Even a strong wind can break the dry, stiff twig. However, a soft green twig will be supple when bent and will not break.*

Could this story be about individuals with inflexible, rigid belief systems? Anyone else?

How could the following metaphor about straws be used?

- Take a paper or plastic straw and bend it. Notice how difficult, if not impossible, it is to drink water through the bent and damaged straw. Even when carefully straightened, the straw's weak area will have creases much like scars. What message might you be sending to someone whose words hurt others? When parents, teachers, and peers ridicule a student, s/he becomes a bent straw. Even with time and healing, the flow continues to be more difficult than before the crippling event.

Sports make wonderful metaphors. For example, a professional woman recently began taking golf lessons. She shared the following instructions from her golf pro.

- "Sight something far in the distance. Even though your ball will not go that far, if you set your sights on a distant object, you will ignore the surrounding distractions and pitfalls such as ponds, trees, and sand pits."

My Friend John. . . and Celebrities

An effective metaphor may begin, *My friend John . . . John* offers the statement that removes the message from you. Notice the following examples from John.

- My friend John said, "Friends treat you the way you treat them first."
- My friend John said, "I found out the hard way, drugs are for dopes!"

A teacher once told the following story to a boy who continually kept a messy desk and backpack. The teachers said,

- One year I had a very messy student who lost papers, broke pencils, and never kept up with assignments. Finally, I said to her, "Don't you realize you are a quality person? Is this any way to treat someone special? Special people don't deserve to live in this mess!"

The student who listened to the story heard the message and without becoming defensive, began to organize materials in a manner more appropriate for a quality, special person.

Use a famous person or a person the students admire to tell the metaphor. For example, Michael Jordon wears Air Jordon basketball shoes. Why do you suppose Nike uses him in television commercials?

To say, Michael Jordon believes education is important, carries a different punch than to say, I want all of you to get a good education.

Smile at each other, smile at your wife, smile at your husband, smile at your children, smile at each other – it doesn't matter who it is —nd that will help you to grow up in greater love for each other.

~*Mother Teresa*

ANCHORING TO MOTIVATE

When you drive down the street and see the McDonald's golden arches, you probably think *hamburger*. Listening to a song played during an early romance brings that partner to mind. Realtors know that the smell of freshly baked bread helps sell homes. In each case, and hundreds more, a feeling or emotion has been bonded by sensory input to a concrete experience. The external experience automatically creates the internal emotional response. Notice how astutely advertisers such as telephone companies create anchors that elicit strong emotions. For example, a lonely grandmother quickly brightens when a telephone call comes from her family. After initially causing you to feel guilty about not contacting your grandmother, the commercial leaves you with warm and fuzzy feelings as you dial the long-distance number.

Sights, sounds, smells, touch, and even tastes constantly occur in classrooms that bond feelings with learning. The connections can be positive or negative. All too often, students bond failure, fear, frustration, and anger with school and with the learning process. Knowing ways to use anchors, (which occur with or without awareness), enables you to create positive bonds or anchors for your students rather than negative ones.

Creating Whole-Class Anchors

Routines and schedules establish anchors and create behaviors that require no reminders. A wise use of routines for predictable aspects of the day saves time, words, and energy and gives students a feeling of security. Consider the following anchors.

- To create anchors for student responsibility, choose one area of the room to write daily assignments and objectives. Color code using the different colors for each assignment. For example, always write the math assignment in green, English in red, and science in blue. During the first few weeks of school, use and explain the anchors consistently. After establishing the connections, students will automatically know where to look to find page numbers and assignments. To strengthen each anchor, get colored paper and cover books with the colors used to write each assignment.
- Play a particular type of music to start the day, another, more mellow piece of music to relax students when the class gets too excited, and a lively march when fatigue sets in. Music establishes feelings that anchor (connect) sound to the behavior you desire.
- Your facial expressions and body language create anchors. Smiling at students, and using high-fives or thumbs up link positive feelings with staying on task or choosing behavior you want to encourage.

- Standing at the front and center of the room with your feet under your shoulders, weight balanced, and hands together, anchors the message, *I am ready for business.*
- Other anchors that automatically solicit desired behaviors include special music for lining up, getting started, or ending class and nonverbal hand signals indicating, *Get quiet, You're on the right track, Start your work,* or *Ask your partner.*

Creating Individual Student Anchors

Getting back spelling tests bloodied with red marks creates a negative anchor (connection) for spelling. Once a negative connection is established, just hearing, "Time for spelling," will probably cause the student to slip into a negative feeling. Years ago, Dr. Madeline Hunter informed teachers that the student who makes a 90 on the test stays motivated to study for the next test. The one who fails dreads the test and avoids even thinking about studying the words. How can this negative anchor be avoided? Read the following examples of individual anchors.

- Letting a student write with a special pen, sit in a favorite chair, or write on colored paper may create positive anchors. One company that specializes in getting pre-service teachers ready for a state teaching exam gives each workshop participant a glittery #2 pencil for taking the test. Although the pre-service teachers are adults, they are encouraged to use their *magic* pencils on the exam day.
- Dignify every student and make certain that each one achieves success (See Anchor Dignity on page 102.) If you must shorten the amount, modify the assignment, spend extra time with the student, or assign a study buddy, you must make certain that every student bonds success with learning.

- When a student who struggles shows the slightest improvement, anchor the feeling of success in three ways:
  - Smile to give the student a visual anchor.
  - Say, *Yes!* to create an auditory bond.
  - Touch the student to establish a tactile anchor.
- During happy, successful times, your smiles, the word *Yes*, and your touch set positive anchors. Repeat these three steps often.
- Once fixed, you can use these anchors to assist a student who is becoming fearful. During a stressful time, touch the student in the same place you anchored the touch, smile as you look the student in the eye, and say, "YES! I know you can learn this. We'll work together till you succeed."
- The anchors recreate former feelings of success, thus promoting a positive resource (belief) within the student. Keep in mind, that if the student believes she will fail, she will. A belief in success empowers one to triumph.

In a different situation, a special education teacher established a secret hand signal for a girl with behavior disorders who constantly interrupted the class with her endless need for love and attention. The teacher's gesture was a nonverbal message; "I care about you. I see that you want to talk to me, and I will get there as quickly as I can." The signal became a powerful anchor to remind the student that the teacher was aware of her and loved her.

Anchor Dignity

Embarrassing a student who offers a wrong answer constitutes one of the quickest ways to anchor fear of failure and feelings of stupidity. While your job includes giving corrective feedback, the way you respond to a wrong answer will make the difference in whether a student continues to try or refuses to participate. The following guidelines suggest ways to dignify an insecure student who gives a different response from the one you expect. Use one of the following statements from Dr. Madeline Hunter's Project BEST.

- "Close! Think about it." (Then give a clue).
- "I can see why you gave that answer. However, the correct answer is…"
- "I know you know the answer. A clue is . . ."
- To the student who raises her hand and then doesn't know the answer say, "You do know the answer. You have forgotten. Provide a clue to help jog the child's memory.
- To help the student who is too shy and insecure to answer in front of the class encourage, "Whisper the answer to me and I'll tell the class what you want to say."
- For the student who never seems to know the answer to any question, work with her ahead of time and rehearse the question and the answer. "I'm planning to call on you to answer this question during reading. Be ready to answer."
- Allow ample time for students to think (for approximately 5 to 7 seconds). Say, "_____ is thinking. Let's be very quiet and help her think."
- If the student is stuck, take the pressure off by saying, "Everyone, get ready to answer this question! Everyone, check with your partners."
- Then return to the stuck student.
- You may ask, "Would you like to pass?" Choosing to pass offers more dignity than asking for help from peers.
- Instead of saying, "This is an easy question," say, "This is a challenge!"
- Change the intonation, and volume of your voice as you ask questions. Make some questions seem mysterious, others exciting.

- Consider buying a small, portable amplifying system so quiet students can speak into a microphone and answer more easily.
- When determining levels of understanding, use positives instead of, "Who needs help?" or "Raise your hand if you have questions." Students will rarely admit either of these. Try the following ideas as alternative ways to check understanding.
  - "I may not have explained clearly. If you're with me, raise your hand."
  - Ask each group or row to confer and make up a group question.
  - Say, "Tell what you do understand!"

Setting Anchors for Yourself

Your enthusiasm motivates and anchors positive feelings both for you and your children. However, when your energy goes down, you will find it difficult to demonstrate your usual lively personality. To combat these downtimes, establish a positive anchor for yourself.

Think of a time when you were very energized, happy, powerful, and confident. Get the picture in your mind. Make it brighter, more colorful, and larger. In your mind, add music if appropriate. Get into the feeling of success. At the peak of recalling and experiencing the memory, give yourself a tactile anchor such as pinching your ear lobe or putting your thumb and little finger together. Choose an anchor that will not be noticeable to others and one that you will not accidentally touch all the time. When losing energy or feeling de-powered, touch your anchor and revive your feelings of power, worth, and confidence.

Wearing various colors or hairstyles may also be anchors for you. On a day when you need energy and excitement, wear a bright color. When stressed, wear soft pink, pale blue, or green. Powerful music may also be a 'power' anchor for you. Use it.

Contaminating Anchors

Be aware that the best anchor, whether for the whole class or an individual student, can become contaminated and even collapse if you weaken or mix the message. If you teach the students that when you hold up your hand (traffic cop stop signal) you mean for them to get quiet, you must be certain to wait for silence and attention before continuing. If, on the other hand, you raise your hand but allow some students to continue moving around, you send a conflicting message that contaminates the anchor. Any time you realize that an anchor that formerly worked, no longer elicits the response you want, you must admit that you allowed the anchor to become contaminated. When this occurs, put the anchor away for a time and introduce a new one.

Special Day Anchors

Exciting days, such as Halloween, just before Christmas, or days when the students stay inside because of bad weather, create a shift to the right side of the brain even for your logical, sequential students. On these days, your regular anchors will not work. To save them from becoming contaminated, use alternate, more dramatic signals until the situation becomes more manageable. For example, if you usually ask for attention by holding up your hand, you may want to change to a clap or soft bell. When life in the classroom returns to normal, return to your original signals.

Dangers of "But"

When working with an individual student, bond positive anchors with positive behavior, and negative anchors with behavior you want to discourage. Do not mix the two. If you give a thumbs-up signal and smile, but add, "This is good, but your handwriting is messy," you contaminate the anchor. The word "but" automatically negates what was said before.

Eliminate "but" from your vocabulary. It is a challenge. Notice the difference in the following statements:

- "You did a good job, but your punctuation is incorrect."
- "Your work looks good, but it is a little late. Speed up the work next time."

Equally important is to make certain your facial expression, body language, gestures, and tone of voice convey the same message as the words you use.

When setting anchors for yourself, stay with the positive. Never bring in the negative. For example, Louise Hay, a national self-esteem expert tells of walking off stage the first time she gave a lecture and saying to herself. *Louise, that was great. It was your first time. You're going to get better and better.* After teaching a class, immediately tell yourself all the things that worked well. Ask your internal critic to wait until you absorb the positive before offering a negative critique or suggesting ways to improve.

Avoiding Negative Anchors

A young teacher took over the class of an older teacher who had been trained in the lecture, drill, and kill method of teaching. Knowing that using the Smart Board usually provides a good way to get the whole class focused, the young teacher developed several lessons using this technology.

Imagine her surprise when the entire class became lethargic and began yawning the instant, she began using the system. It didn't matter how interesting her lesson was, the time of day, or the subject being taught. The students were anchored to going to sleep when the technology started.

It became necessary for the young teacher to avoid the Smart Board for several days and use charts and chalkboards to teach her lessons. In time, she re-introduced the Smart Board by asking the class to stand and march to music as she briefly displayed her lessons.

In a different situation, a third-grade teacher wondered why her new class was difficult to teach. As she passed the room of the students' former second-grade teacher, she heard the teacher yelling at the class. The third-grade teacher realized that the students were so negatively anchored to yelling that they immediately turned off any loud voice. Even though the third-grade teacher usually spoke loudly, she resolved to spend the remainder of the year speaking very softly to the students.

Collapsing Anchors

You may have a student who developed a very negative anchor and association with a subject. For example, every time you mention math, you notice the student becoming tense. The student may appear to shrink behind the book and avoid making eye contact with you. Since this fear creates a barrier to learning, you want to collapse the negative anchor.

Just as you use visual and auditory sensations along with positive feelings to create positive bonds, you will use the same principle in reverse to collapse a negative anchor.

Ask the student to create a movie in which she sees herself doing math. However, instead of keeping the movie inside her head (as you do to create a positive anchor), encourage her to imagine setting up a screen somewhere in the room. As she watches the movie from a third-person perspective, ask her to give a third-person description of what is happening by saying to herself, "She is getting out her math book. She is dreading this class. She is avoiding looking at the teacher so she will not get called on for an answer."

Once the student establishes the scene as an observable event outside herself, she has already achieved some measure of objectivity. Build on this by encouraging her to:

- remove the color from the movie
- change from a movie to a still picture
- put a frame around the picture and reduce the size of the picture
- move the picture to the far side of the room, then outside, down the block, and finally out of town
- lower the sound
- muffle the sound
- distort both the sound and the picture

Encourage the student to disassociate the negative feelings with math. The term *disassociate* brings understandable concern to teachers who know that many students, particularly males, disassociate feelings and emotions much of the time. The purpose of viewing a past event objectively from the third person is to encourage the student to see the situation for what it is: an old memory stuck in present emotions.

Setting Standards

Imagine the opportunities you seek, and they will become reality. Whatever you can do, or dream you can do, begin it. Boldness has genius, power, and magic in it.

~Goethe

Sending An "I" Message

Dr. Thomas Gordon, a psychologist, founded and became president of Effectiveness Training Associates, a nationwide training program for parents, teachers, and others working with children. Dr. Gordon's training programs and his clinical practice rely on a win-win philosophy that emphasizes the rights of everyone involved in a situation.

Mastering the dual communication skills of sending and responding to messages offers a powerful method for creating winning classrooms.

When You Own the Problem

When you feel upset, you own the problem. You have a right and responsibility to take care of your needs and wants. You also have a responsibility to communicate in a way that gets the message across without causing others to feel guilty or fearful. The goal is to accept responsibility for your feelings without blaming others. Read through the following examples.

As you teach, you notice Travis carving his initials on a desk. Travis loves carving. He is enjoying himself.

Who owns the problem? You own the problem. You feel upset. Travis feels contented.

Sally comes to school 30 minutes late every morning. She interrupts class and misses the directions for independent work. Later, Sally wants you to give instructions to her privately.

Who owns the problem? You own the problem. Giving individual directions wastes your time. Sally feels happy about coming in late and enjoys your one-on-one attention.

Sending an "I" Message

No matter how right or justified your anger may be, if you cannot communicate in a way that invites receptivity, you waste time and energy. When sending a communication that could be interpreted as negative, Gordon suggests using an "I" message to convey, that I am responsible for what I feel. I am sharing my feelings and my desires with you. The message avoids blame or accusations such as, *You are making me feel….* In truth, no one can make you feel anything.

Directions for Phrasing an "I" Message

Think of a behavior that causes a problem for you. Since you own the problem, you must initiate the communication. Using the following starters, develop a clear and effective "I" message.

- "When I see/hear/notice . . ." (name a behavior)
- "I feel . . ." (be honest)
- "I want you to please . . ." (be specific and brief)

Your only purpose at this point is to name the specific behavior, state how you feel, and suggest what you want. You have no guarantees that you will get what you want, but you have improved your chances. Keep in mind that people tend to overreact when attacked or when told they are wrong. However, the same individuals may react favorably when told how you feel. If the recipient gets defensive, remind him/her that you have a right to feel what you feel.

The hardest part of sending an "I" message is to stop talking once the message has been sent. Preaching, judging, ordering, or warning destroy the beauty and simplicity of open communication.

Homework

- "When homework isn't done . . ." (Description)
- "I'm afraid you won't lean," (Feeling)
- "I want you to finish." (Request)

Shouting

- "When I hear shouting," (Description)
- "It hurts my ears." (Feeling)
- "Please yell outside when playing." (Request)

Game Pieces

- "When game pieces get scattered," (Description)
- "I suspect they will get lost." (Feeling)
- "Please keep all the game pieces together." (Request)

Nothing creates resentment and resistance faster than attacks and commands. Avoid orderings, warnings, sermons, and judgments. Consider the problems with the examples below.

Negative Examples

- "Stop talking!" (Ordering)
- "How many times have I told you? Next time . . ." (Warning)
- "You should know better. Shame on you." (Preaching)
- "You're being bad." (Judging)

Ordering

- "You're fighting again!" (Description)
- "Stop fighting now!" (Ordering)
- Feeling: "You're driving me crazy!" (Feeling – but not a healthy feeling)

Warning

- "Your desk is a mess." (Description)
- "If you know what's good for you, you'll . . ." (Warning)
- "I think you are lazy." (Feeling)

Preaching

- "Are you still talking?" (Description)
- "You should know better." (Preaching)
- "What a waste of my time." (Feeling)

Judgment

- "You called me a rude name." (Description)
- "Good girls don't talk like that." (Judgment)
- "I'm ashamed of you." (Feeling)

Who Gets the First Turn?

Once you have shared your feelings and desires, the person receiving your message may have strong emotions. Just as you wanted the student to listen, the student now wants to be heard and understood by you. When students have strong negative feelings, you can help diffuse the feelings by using Active Listening.. See Active Listening on page 45

Who gets to share feelings and make a request first? The child who wants to send an I message to you goes first.

By using Active Listening, you will let the child know you are listening, you care, and that with help, you believe that the child will identify a solution.

Whatever action we take may influence the course of civilization. The decision of whether to praise or punish a single child may have vast consequences.

REDIRECTING STUDENTS

You must always keep two ideals in mind. Your first responsibility is to nurture and teach children. A second and equal responsibility is to make certain no one stops you from teaching or prevents children from learning. Individual children may choose not to learn. Certainly, you will spare no effort to motivate and believe in each student in your charge. After you have done what you can to reach an unmotivated student, you must realize that the student has a human right to make poor choices.

However, once the student crosses the line and begins to interfere with your ability to teach or the opportunity for other children to learn you have an enormous responsibility to actively protect the class from her disruptive behavior. In this section, you will consider several non-punishing ways to handle serious challenges in the classroom.

Logical Consequences

When students participate in creating behavior guidelines and consequences, they comply more readily than if the teacher arbitrarily sets rules and punishments. The better the consequences fit the behavior (whether negative or positive), the greater understanding students will have.

One of the most mistaken beliefs in teaching and in parenting is that punishment is necessary. *Spare the rod and spoil the child* has long been quoted by experts. Consider the following story about punishment.

In an inner-city school, three fifth-grade boys decided to decorate the boys' restroom with their choice of graffiti. Enraged teachers and administrators insisted on knowing who did the graffiti. No one would either tell on the students or admit the deed. The teachers decided to punish all fifth graders in the class by taking away free time for a week.

A young student teacher noticed that even those who normally responded well to her suddenly became uncooperative and negative. After investigating, she discovered that the entire class felt angry about the punishment. Students bonded together. Teachers had become a common enemy.

As an alternative to punishment, teachers could have stated matter-of-factly that the restroom had to be painted. Teachers could also have assured the boys that they still cared about those who left graffiti. However, teachers insisted that the community property must be repaired. No anger. No threats. No punishment. In fact, the teachers and all class members would be willing to join them in painting and cleaning up their school property.

Time would indeed be taken from academics. The project would probably also be fun for everyone involved. Does making the consequence meaningful and even playful mean it couldn't work? What larger lessons could students learn from working together to repair the damage? Possibilities include:

- We are all in this together (teachers too).
- Every act is tied to a consequence.
- Cooperating is better than fighting.
- There is no need to be angry. We all make mistakes.
- Each individual is responsible for the good of all.

The following examples demonstrate the differences between natural consequences (which occur with no action from the teacher) and logical consequences (which require some participation on the part of the teachers).

Natural Consequence

- Forgets lunch — goes without
- Does not turn in homework— gets a zero
- Stays up too late — falls asleep in school

Logical Consequence

- Disrupts class — moves away from his group
- Spins his ruler —loses his ruler
- Refuses to participate —works alone (It probably does not matter if the child prefers to work alone or not. Unless the purpose is to work cooperatively, the consequence is neither to reward nor to punish. The consequence is designed for each child to master the information.

Consequences & Punishment

When working with students, you have everything to gain from an atmosphere of *let's grow and learn together* and everything to lose from an environment of, *it's them against me*. Punishment frequently appears unfair to students and creates resentment that often leads to more negative behavior. In your classrooms, students outnumber you, they are faster, more energetic, meaner, and even smarter than you are! You, the teacher, will never win in an adversarial situation. Below are some examples of events and ways parents and teachers often punish children.

Event	Punishment
Bob hits Tom.	Bob gets spanked.
Mary cheats on a test.	Mary goes to the office.
Tom forgets his homework	Tom misses free time for a week.
Jim leaves things on the floor.	Jim sits in time-out for ten minutes.

Notice that each punishment requires time and energy. In addition, students rarely understand the relationships between behaviors and punishments. In each of the cases above, students probably resent the punishment.

In addition, unintentional consequences may create more problems than the punishment hoped to solve. For example:

- When Bob got spanked, he decided that hitting was OK if you're big. He became a bully.
- The visit to the principal's office frightened Mary and she never trusted her principal again.
- Tom decided to use his time-outs to finish his homework. The practice of doing homework never got established.
- Jim did not relate his ten-minute time-outs for losing his things. He continued to leave things scattered around the room, as he wasted his time-outs.

In the following chart, based on the behaviors above, the consequences seem logical. Thus, they are easier for students to understand.

Event	Natural Consequence
Bob hits Tom.	Tom no longer wants to play with Bob.
Mary cheats on a test.	Mary retakes the test.
Tom forgets homework.	Toms misses free time until his work is finished.
Jim leaves things on the floor.	Jim's things accidentally get thrown away.

Logical consequences match behaviors and make sense to students. Another advantage is that consequences usually require no extra effort or time on your part. However, solution thinking is even better than consequences. Notice the use of solutions instead of punishments or consequences in the following examples.

Event	Possible Solution	What Jim Learned
Jim talks out.	Jim keeps a tally of the number of times he talks.	Jim realizes how often he talks out. He sets goals for himself. The goals belong to Jim so he wants to keep them.
Betty rolls her eyes and sighs loudly.	Betty writes a description of her behavior and lists three new ways to describe her feelings.	Betty begins to use her new ideas to provide feedback without offending others.
Joe is failing.	A volunteer study buddy system is set up for Joe.	Joe notices that he can learn with a little help. Motivation increases. The tutors also improve.

Neither logical nor natural consequences involve anger. In fact, often the only difference between consequence and punishment is the attitude of the teacher or parent. The words, "If you continue to disrupt the other students, you will move to another area of the room," can be delivered as nothing more than a factual message or can be said through clenched teeth and a tight stomach. Even if you smile when feeling angry, students know the difference.

Proximity

Proximity, which means physically moving closer to a student, offers one of the easiest and most powerful redirecting procedures available. When moving beside a student isn't enough, you can add even more proximity by touching the student's desk or even touching the student. A few students resist being touched and should be respected. With these students, touch their desks, books, or papers instead. When assisting a student with hyperactivity and a short attention span, make the most of proximity by adding the following steps.

- Move beside the student who is off task.
- Instead of immediately moving away, stay beside or behind the student. You may notice that the hyperactive student will:
  - hold her breath
  - stop the undesirable behavior
  - pretend to engage in the assigned task
- Stay with the student until you see her start to breathe normally and start working.
- Once she is engaged in the task, back away from the student.

With most students with attention problems, your proximity interrupts the negative behavior and puts the student in a neutral state while waiting for you to leave. As soon as you walk away, the student resumes the previous off-task activity. By staying long enough for the student to get started with the work, you have lengthened the time the student will stay on task.

Offering Choices

When working with any child, remember the power of choices. Allowing a student to determine choices reduces resistance and promotes self-responsibility. For all but the most serious situations, create choices that offer positive and acceptable alternatives. Saying, "You may listen to the information or take a sad face home," really offers no choice at all. Stretch your creative thinking to offer legitimate choices that do not involve punishment and will be acceptable to both you and the student. Keep in mind that you do not have to punish a student to effectively redirect. The following examples suggest types of acceptable choices.

- You may listen or move slightly away from the group.
- You may do work now or during your free time.
- You may sit at your desk or move to the learning center to do your work.
- You may have a snack while studying if you choose.
- You may listen to quiet instrumental music while you work, or you may study quietly.

Offer choices that you can live with. A child may say, "I don't want either _____ or _____. I want _____." You reply "That is not one of your choices. However, you may (repeat your options)." Make certain you stick with the two choices you offered unless the student suggests an idea that you believe is valid and as acceptable as yours.

Strengthening Choices

At an early age, children begin to understand choices. For example, one child snatches a toy from another child who immediately begins to cry. You say "We have a problem. Joy is crying. Both of you want the same toy. How can we solve this?"

Initially, you will probably need to suggest a few possibilities, such as, "You could wait until Joy has finished playing with this toy. You could offer her a different one as a trade. You could look for a toy just like the one she has. You could play together." You may finally say, "I see we can't find an answer. Until we can think of a solution, I'll keep this toy until later."

Strengthen the importance of making good choices by asking, "Did you make a good choice when you snatched the toy from your friend?" Regardless of the answer, ask, "Did your choice make you happy?"

Alternatives for Expressing Anger

At a calm time, offer the following alternatives to an angry student who hurts himself, others, or property. Say, "It's OK to be angry. I am not willing for you to hit, but I am willing for you to show me how angry you are by _____."

- demonstrating anger with clay (kinesthetic)
- drawing a picture showing what the anger looks like (visual)
- talking into a tape recorder to describe the anger (auditory)
- writing and destroying an anger letter (tactile)

If you encourage a student to use alternatives to express anger and/or negative feelings, you must accept the message and the delivery without withdrawal of love and support for the student. You may not censor the student's words, pictures, or actions as long as the student expresses feelings without causing injury or damage.

Apologies and Making Amendments

Angry students often hurt or offend other students or teachers. Insisting that a student apologize or give compliments when the student is still angry teaches insincerity. Preferably, offer some suggestions and choices for making amends. Then allow the student to choose one that feels right. You may also want to encourage the angry student to choose a time (perhaps a day or two later) to help the hurt individual feel better. Ideas for making amends include:

- giving smiles, and greetings
- getting supplies, books, and materials for the student who was hurt
- eating lunch together
- giving a sincere compliment
- agreeing not to repeat the behavior
- giving a sincere apology
- telling a joke to the hurt student

No one has the right to hurt others. When hurt feelings occur, action must be taken to create healing. By allowing the student who did the hurting to choose a way to correct the situation, you encourage personal responsibility. This is far different than insisting on an immediate apology from a student still fuming.

Understanding Conflicts

Help your students resolve conflicts in ways that create winning solutions for everyone involved. First, guide them to understand the nature of conflicts and the benefits of solutions. A class discussion about the meaning of conflict will help students understand that:

- everyone has conflicts at from time to time
- anger is a natural reaction when life does not work the way we want it to
- certain ways of expressing anger work better than other ways

Solutions that work must meet the needs of everyone involved. After discussing possible solutions to various conflicts, ask students to:

- draw pictures of personal conflicts on large index cards
- draw pictures of possible solutions on the backs of the same cards

Older students may also choose to write about their conflicts as well as ideas for solutions. Help students understand the futility of seeking solutions while still angry. A cool-down time may benefit all concerned.

Conflict Resolution

Teach students to use the following mediation model. Initially, you want to be the mediator. If you take time early in the year to guide students in conflict mediation, students will be able to apply the principles later in the school year without your assistance.

Wait until students are calm enough to talk and to listen. Ask, "Do you want to work out a solution or do you only want to blame someone else?" Explain that each student involved in the conflict will have an opportunity to talk and to be heard. Until one person finishes, the other student must remain quiet and listen. Mediate for the students.

- Tell the first student, "State what you want, how you feel, and why you feel the way you do." Sample statements follow:
  - "I want the book."
  - "I feel frustrated and panicky about time."
  - "I need the book to finish my assignment before 3:00 so I can go to football practice. "
- The second student restates the message to make certain that the communication was received accurately.
  - "You want the book now."
  - "You're frustrated because you're running out of time."
  - "You want to get the work done now so you can go to football practice."
- The first person either confirms or clarifies the communication.
- Reverse roles and repeat the sequence.
- Ask students if they want to find a solution.
- Encourage each student to suggest three possible solutions.
- Insist that students agree on the best solution(s).
- Expect students to shake hands to confirm their mutual agreement.
- Congratulate the students on their winning solution.

Courtesy Chair

The Courtesy Chair offers a consequence that keeps the disruptive student in the room and controls personal behavior. Although slightly different from the traditional time-out, both seek to disrupt the disruption.

- Establish one to three chairs in the room that serve as courtesy chairs.
- Explain the purpose of the courtesy chairs - to offer students a chance to think about behavior. Make certain the students understand that the chairs are not intended as punishment.

- Demonstrate the signal you plan to use if you want a student to move to the courtesy chair. The signal needs to be nonverbal so you can continue teaching without interrupting your lesson.
- Allow students to decide when to return to their seats. Say, "I don't know how long you need to sit in the chair to be ready to . . . You are the only one who can know when you are ready to try again."
- As soon as a student returns, greet the student warmly and say, "I'm so glad you're ready to participate. Welcome back!"

If the same student begins the negative behavior again, silently indicate a return to the courtesy chair. Some students need to go back to the chair many times. If you

continue to disrupt the negative behavior and continue to teach, you are succeeding. Likewise, since each visit to the courtesy chair reminds the child of the desired behavior, your student is learning.

However, even the best ideas can backfire! In one classroom, children who went to courtesy chairs barely touched the seats of chairs before insisting they had thought about their behaviors and wanted to learn. Suddenly, more confusion erupted from the rapid coming and going than the original behaviors. The teacher needed to change tactics.

For these children, a more traditional approach seemed appropriate. Always keep your purpose and goal in mind: to teach and to ensure that children learn. When a disruption occurs, stop the behavior with as little interruption to the lesson as possible.

Some students do not know the difference between acceptable social behavior and behavior that will get them in trouble. Distinguish and model appropriate behavior for them. Never assume students know how to act and never accept the unacceptable. Allowing students to get away with unacceptable behavior at school sets them up for later problems with social, personal, and business relationships.

Time-out

If a self-monitored courtesy chair fails to work, you may want to create a more traditional time-out location. While introducing a time-our space, spend time discussing the causes, needed changes, and desired outcomes with the entire class. Each class and each age will have unique behaviors. For that reason, ask each class to create a list of unhelpful behaviors. Likewise, ask children to determine actions to replace those that the group decides are unacceptable. Below, you can read ideas to consider.

Behaviors That Cause Time-out	New Behaviors to Try in the Future
Arguing with another student	Say, "We can agree to disagree." "We can ask the teacher for help."
Breaking rules when playing a game	Read the rules ahead of time. Agree to follow the rules.
Interrupting the speaker	Raise a hand to request permission to be called on
Bothering students who are trying to study	Either stay at your desk or walk quietly without interrupting others
Jumping on the backs of classmates when walking down the stairs.	Walk safely while going down the stairs.
Refusing to leave a learning center	Leave a learning center when the time ends

One expert suggests that after two minutes, the teacher joins the child in a time-out space. The expert claims that after two minutes, children begin to create new issues.

Based on class discussions, the teacher will type one list of behaviors that cause time-outs and a second list of more resourceful actions to take. Use these pre-determined lists to ask, "Why did I ask you to go to time-out?" The second question will follow, "What do you plan to do next time?"

Once you join time-out, you need to process the behaviors and goals as quickly as possible. If the child identifies the reason she was asked to go to time-out and can indicate a new plan, she returns to her seat. Nothing more needs to be done.

If a child cannot answer your two questions, start the timer for an additional two minutes. Continue at two-minute intervals until the child can respond to your two questions. Do not feel you are failing. Every two minutes you are reminding and reinforcing expected behavior.

- After each additional two minutes, the teacher will ask, "Why are you in time-out?"
- If the student promptly describes the behavior that created the time-out, ask, "What will you do in the future?"
- If the student reacts angrily or refuses to state the behavior, say, "I see you're not ready." Begin the timer again for another two minutes.

You will probably feel keeping track of two-minute intervals takes too much learning time. However, if you establish the precedent in the first weeks of a new school year, your investment in consequences will pay off for the remainder of the year.

For the first two to four weeks, concentrate on setting expectations, establishing procedures, and letting the children know you care. Teachers who spend the first few weeks concentrating on behaviors and expectations will easily make up for lost time the remainder of the year by encountering fewer disruptions. Even with a loving and firm start, you will occasionally get tested. When the inevitable tests occur, take time to reaffirm the consequences for unacceptable behavior.

Learn or Leave

Reserve your use of Learn or Leave for a student who continues to disrupt the learning opportunity for other students even in the Courtesy Chair or Time-out. This student continues to prevent you from teaching and blocks others from learning.

Students who do not want to learn and who ruin the learning process for others will be given a choice: to learn or to leave.

Your intention continues to be preserving the learning climate and maintaining your right to teach rather than to punish. Student choice is the key. Students who continually disrupt are choosing to be asked to leave. Only when a disruptive student chooses to learn will negative behavior cease. You can encourage, but not force a choice for learning.

The most valuable way to reinforce the importance of staying in your classroom is to make certain your lessons include movement. Keep what you say short. Keep the children involved in doing something interesting. Music, art, stories, and any physical involvement are your most powerful avenues to link pleasure and learning.

Where to Send a Child

Decide in advance where to send the student. Choices to consider include:
- the hall outside your room
- the counselor's office
- the library or
- another teacher's room (teachers often offer this for one another)

Some schools offer in-school suspension with paid staff observation and assistance. A wonderful alternative would be Glasser's Quality Room (page 2)3 where a teacher or counselor suggests and rehearses appropriate behaviors. None of these options should be presented as punishments but rather as solutions for disruptions in classrooms.

Many principals expect teachers to handle problems and do not appreciate frequent referrals to the office. For this reason, reserve office referrals for the most difficult cases. There was a time when the major responsibility of a school principal was to handle behavior problems. Since principals have become inundated with paperwork, meetings, and responsibilities to upper administration, they have little time to handle classroom problems. In addition, the new rationale is that when you send a student to the office you are communicating, *I cannot handle this child. I give up.* The downside is that many teachers feel unsupported.

Maintaining Management of Behaviors

The solution for maintaining your authority as a teacher requires that regardless of where you send the child, you must either take responsibility for the consequence, or you must co-own responsibility for a logical or natural consequence. If your counselor takes over and establishes a reasonable consequence without including you, the child will only feel answerable to the counselor.

If you and the counselor (or a teacher receiving your child) find a time and way to communicate agreement and compliance with a consequence, you share authority.

The front porch of a portable is tempting but may not be a safe place to send a child depending on your school situation and environment. Sample wording for learn or leave is offered below.

- "I want to teach. The other children want to learn. I want you to learn also. If you do not want to learn and will not allow others to learn, please leave the room. The choice is yours."
- "If you choose to leave, I will note the time you are out of the classroom and you will make up the class during free time, recess, or after school."
- Tell the student, "You may rejoin the class when you are ready to learn and to help others learn. You only make up the time you choose to be out of the classroom."
  - There is no attitude of punishment when students are in control.
  - Most students understand your logic.
  - Allowing the student to determine when to return to the group puts the student, not you, in charge of learning.
- When the student decides to return, welcome her by saying, "I see you are ready to learn. Good for you."
- If the student regresses to disruptive behavior, repeat the process.

Therefore, a child who spends five minutes out of the room only loses five minutes of free time or recess and may join the others when the time ends. Doesn't this seem logical? Forcing a child to miss the entire recess period amounts to punishment, makes no sense to the child, and takes away the child's physiological and psychological needs for movement and play. In effect, if you take away all recess and/or outside time, you are creating a new set of problems by restricting physical exercise.

Requirements for Each Removal

Regardless of which, if any system you use, responsibility will always return to you, the teacher.

- Other than using a nonverbal signal for a child to move, the Courtesy Chair requires the least amount of work on you.

- Time-out requires a class discussion to determine the behaviors that typically require a student to move to time-out. In addition, a similar list will describe suitable replacement behaviors. Finally, you will visit with children in Time-Out every two minutes until the child can express a reason for Time-Out and appropriate replacement behavior.
- Learn or Leave requires identifying a place for a student to go, recording time-out of the classroom, establishing make-up time, and monitoring makeup time.

Quality Room

Please refer to the Quality Room, Glasser's concept for removing students from the classroom, on page 32.

Teachers who send children to the Quality Room to punish them will be disappointed. Likewise, those who send children to the room to get work done will be equally unhappy.

However, teachers who appreciate having an adult who has time to actively teach new social behaviors will be grateful to have access to a Quality Room. Keep in mind that a Quality Room accomplishes two goals. First, you have disrupted the behavior that is keeping you from teaching and keeping other children from learning. Second, the child demonstrating the misbehavior receives feedback, instruction, and rehearsal of new behaviors from a caring adult.

DIVERSITY

We are all pencils in the hand of God.

~Mother Theresa

FOUR BASIC TYPES

Both Lee Canter and Rudolph Dreikurs describe four types of challenging students in our classrooms. Canter and Dreikurs refer to these students as feeling inadequate, needing attention, wanting to control others, and seeking revenge. In each case, the student's behavior indicates a deep need. Any inappropriate behavior points to a mistaken goal that the student believes will bring relief. Recall Glasser's five basic needs and his belief that all behaviors are chosen with the expectation of getting needs met. (See Quality Schools on page 19.)

Mistaken goals include wanting to: avoid the learning task, gain attention, take control, and get revenge. A need not met at one level escalates to the next. Ultimately, if real needs remain unmet, the student becomes hostile and seeks revenge.

Once you identify and respond to the student's real need, the behavior begins to diminish. Although logical consequences are often appropriate, punishment tends to increase the neediness, and undesirable behaviors escalate. Instead of trying to control students, seek to identify and respond to the need that drives the behavior. Keep in mind, *every behavior is meaningful.* Ask yourself, *What is the need that causes this behavior?*

Although you will usually be able to identify one of the four mistaken goals, students do not fit into tidy boxes and often exhibit a combination of mistaken goals and behaviors. As you read each of the individual descriptions below, keep in mind that you may see overlapping and even escalating behaviors in children with unmet needs.

The Avoidance/Inadequate Student

A capable student who avoids work because of feelings of inadequacy causes great frustration to teachers and parents. This is not the student with learning disabilities, low intelligence, or emotional disturbance. You know the student can do the work. The student, who believes the task is too hard, tries to avoid facing the task. This student's real *need is to build inner confidence.* Until the inner need is met, symptoms will continue. The student who feels inadequate often does the following:

- avoids getting started
- gives up quickly
- thinks or says things like, *I'm stupid,* or *This is too hard for me*
- whines or cries

Your Feelings

Some days you may feel irritated; most days you feel sad for the student and hopelessly want to help. You may experience situations in which you help too much and do most of the work. This reinforces the student's belief in inadequacy. The student thinks, *Yep, I'm hopeless. The teacher did this for me.* Your feelings provide a predictable guide for determining the student's deep need. Notice that when the student feels pitiful and hopeless, you too begin to feel sad, hopeless, and pitiful for the student.

In a Crisis

Sometimes, you have little time and many other students' needs to consider. In a moment of crisis with an avoidance student, keep the following ideas in mind.

- Say, "I know you feel discouraged. Add Let's get started together."
- Cover all but one part of an assignment.
- Acknowledge or reward each part.
- Add one new, short part at a time.
- Look for successes and tell the student, "I knew you could do it!"

If the child continues to resist, you may choose to say, "Do it anyway," or, "You can do it now or during. . . " As you work with the student, it is important to avoid coaxing as well as pity.

Meeting the Real Need for Self-Confidence

Dr. Madeline Hunter warns that a student who constantly fails becomes unmotivated. For this reason, you want to do everything possible to ensure a series of successes for the student who feels inadequate. One successful completion will not meet the need. The student who feels inadequate probably came to this conclusion over some time and many failures. Only regular, long-term, daily success will reprogram the student's attitude. The following ideas help build confidence and overcome feelings of inadequacy.

- Modify the assignment either by altering the level of difficulty or the amount required. Continue to modify assignments until the student's confidence allows a slow increase in difficulty or amount.
- Invite the student to join in solving the problem. Ask, "How can we solve this?"
- Teach the use of self-talk, "I can do it."

Actions That Escalate Negative Behavior

Nagging the student will escalate the behaviors you do not want. When working with a student who feels inadequate, omit:

- giving pity
- doing the work for the student
- nagging the student
- punishing the student
- asking, "What's wrong with you?"
- comparing the student to others

The Attention-Needy Student

Many students come to school with a need for love and acceptance. Their behavior, designed to get your attention, irritates and annoys. Their real need, to be loved, goes unfulfilled. The only way for a needy student to truly heal is through *self*-acceptance and *self*-love. The first step toward that inner healing may come from your positive redirecting.

Behaviors of the Student

The student who needs attention and love generally behaves in ways that seem innocent enough but distract you and the other students. The attention-needy student may:

- tap a pencil
- hum at inappropriate times
- rock back in her chair
- walk around the room
- interrupt others
- lose pencils, papers, books
- pull on your sleeve
- get jealous of the attention you give to other students
- need your attention when you are busy

Your Feelings

Even when you realize the student exhibits a real need, you often feel annoyed. You wonder, *How many times have I told Sam to stop interrupting me?*

Suggestions When in Crisis

When behaviors occur in the middle of class or at a time when you cannot stop and discuss behavior with the student, the following sequence makes a significant difference.

- Keep doing what you are doing.
- Avoid saying the student's name or looking the student in the eye during negative behavior. This will be enormously challenging.
- Without saying the student's name or making eye contact, give the student a hug or gentle back rub during negative behavior.
- Make certain to touch this needy child gently and slowly. Your goal is to wordlessly convey, *I am working with other children and I still care about you.*
- Avoid patting, ruffling hair, pinching ears playfully, and moving quickly. These behaviors have a place but not now with this student.

All teachers, especially males, must take care of themselves as they work with students. Touching, which is so needed by students, can result in questions from anxious parents and administrators. Always use common sense, be certain to touch non-sexually, and always make certain other people are around.

Suggestions for Later

At a later time, do everything possible to build self-acceptance and self-love in the student.

- As often as possible, name each positive behavior the student exhibits using very specific words. "You did row one in math. You can feel good about this hard work you did by yourself."
- Teach the student to use positive self-talk. An appropriate example of self-talk is to affirm, "I love and respect myself and am loved by others". Although not a magic fix for a student who needs love and attention, affirmations offer a start toward self-healing.
- During a calm time say, I'm not willing for you to interrupt me. I have many other students to teach. "Let's think of a secret signal we can use when you need attention."
- The attention-needy student may decide to communicate feelings of need by raising a thumb. You respond by sending a similar signal, which you and the student predetermined to mean, *I care about you, and I'll spend time with you as quickly as possible.*
- Acknowledge appropriate behavior by using eye contact and the student's name. Always appreciate positive behavior. If *positive* behavior is ignored, it will go away.

Actions That Escalate Feelings of Inadequacy

Needy students frequently get negative feedback for their behaviors. The negative feedback gains attention for the wrong reason. It also deepens the feelings of need and a conviction that I am not loved. Therefore, avoid:

- saying, *Don't interrupt*
- rejecting the student
- yelling at the student
- looking at the student during negative attention-getting behavior

The Bossy, Control Student

Nothing you say or do satisfies the bossy, control student. Moreover, the bossy student demonstrates an outward need to correct and control other students. When a substitute teacher comes, this student is merciless! The real inner need, to feel safe enough to give up control and trust others, hides beneath an assertive exterior.

Perhaps the student comes from a home in which no adult handles life responsibly. Some children learn very early to switch roles with one or both parents and assume more responsibility than a healthy child should carry. Their bossy, controlling attitude typically:

- defies authority, argues
- says, *I won't and you can't make me*
- confronts and talks back
- bosses other students
- refuses to comply
- makes rude comments
- says, *You are doing it wrong!*

Your Feelings

You feel challenged and angry. The bossy, controlling student is not pitiful and wants much more than attention. The student desires to run the show and challenge your authority as a teacher.

In a Crisis

When challenged in front of other students, parents, teachers, or administrators, you are in a crisis. If not used too often, you may find it helpful to say:

- "I want to be certain I understand. You are telling me you will not do what I asked. Is this correct? If the student replies yes, you will respond by saying, That is useful information. We will handle this at a later time." Continue teaching.

Follow through with the next sequence of steps. Give the class a simple task to do and motion nonverbally for the student to follow you out of the classroom.

- It is vital to remove the bossy student from the class. This student will strongly resist if confronted in the presence of peers. Saving face is vital to a student who hopes to control others. Talking softly in front of the others does not work. Other students will hear, or the control student will believe they will hear.
- Once out of the classroom, communicate in a friendly way.
  - Touch the student.
  - Look the student in the eye, say the student's name, and add, "I'm not willing for you to . . ."
  - Offer choices, "You may do or _____."

Suggestions for Later

At a later time, assign positive leadership tasks to the student. This student needs to feel powerful. A useful job offers the student a feeling of being in control and, thus, being safe. Examples include:

- letting the student be a noise monitor
- putting the student in charge of checking out important materials

If logical or natural consequences are needed, use them quickly. Avoid multiple warnings.

Actions That Escalate Negative Behavior

The student who wants to control the classroom enjoys and gets a payoff from a struggle with you. If you show anger or let the student know that you feel challenged, the student wins the battle. You are not teaching, you are arguing. The student gains control! Remember not to:

- resist the student
- argue, fight, or force the student to comply
- embarrass the student in front of others

The Hostile Student Who Wants Revenge

Some authorities believe that three to five percent of the students in your classroom will not respond to any of your management efforts. The student who comes to school angry at the world and ready for revenge exhibits behavior that frightens teachers and students. Standard classroom management procedures will not work when confronted with a student in a fit of rage. In fact, standard practices such as using proximity may not even be safe. Immediate, firm, assertive, yet kind action must be used.

Behaviors of the Student

The outward manifestation of the hostile student is rage. The outward goal, to get revenge for real or perceived pain in the student's life, covers the *inner need for emotional healing*. Remember, *The amount of pain a student creates is a measure of the pain carried inside.* The hostile student wanting revenge:

- willfully destroys property
- hurts other students
- engages in substance abuse
- pouts throws tantrums
- is openly rude to parents/teachers
- screams, spits, curses
- uses self-destructive behavior
- fights, lies, steals

Your Feelings

When an angry, hostile student erupts in your classroom, you feel fear and tremendous stress. You may feel either deeply hurt, enraged, or both. Natural instinct wants to hurt back. However, this student's behavior indicates enormous and tragic pain. Hurting back in the form of anger or punishment only adds to the pain in the student, which, in turn, adds to the student's desire to hurt self or others.

Witnessing an out-of-control situation frightens students, and even though uninvolved, creates anxiety. For the sake of the children in the class, as well as the hostile student, you cannot afford to show either hurt or anger.

Things NOT To Do in a Crisis

Do not scream or attempt to force the child to do anything. Stay calm. Use your self-talk. Help the other students feel safe. The children look to you to get the situation under control and to take care of the crisis for them. It is more important to remember what to avoid than what to do. Remember not to:

- show anger
- argue, debate, or bargain with the student
- hurt back
- use proximity
- state an "I" message (the hostile student will be glad you feel upset)

Things To Do In a Crisis

In a moment of crisis, use your self-talk to stay as calm as possible. In addition:

- Immediately use your most severe logical consequence, which is to remove the student from the classroom.
- In some cases, it may be easier to remove the class from the hostile student.

If the student will not cooperate, ask the class to walk calmly to the library (or to another safe space) and wait for you. Your objective is to remove the other students from the classroom. As the class leaves, call for assistance. Quietly stay with the hostile student until help arrives. Your goal is to calm the student and to do your best to prevent harm to the child or yourself. Forget about damage to school property.

Suggestions for Later

Once the student leaves the room and the class has been restored to order, spend some time thinking and writing.

- As soon as possible, document everything that was said and happened. If there were witnesses, ask them to document the behavior with you. Sign and date the document.
- Write, *Three things I love about this student are* . . . Writing is very important. The three things that you write must be more significant than, she has beautiful eyes.
- Look for patterns of events that precede outbursts. These prior events, called antecedents, can sometimes be altered or avoided to prevent the problem. For example, does the angry student tend to lose control at predictable times of day, after or before certain classes, or when encountering specific students?
- Are some assignments more stressful than others? Are there games in which the student cannot control emotions?

When the Student Returns

When the student returns to the classroom, you must gain rapport and trust. Remember that your intentions create the only difference in logical consequences and punishment. This mental and emotional shift requires a bit of inner work on your head and your heart. Mentally, say, *This child hurts very badly. How can I love this one who seems so unlovable?*

If the student breaks windows while angry, she must repair the windows or pay to have them fixed. If you announce in a loud, angry voice "You will pay for the damages," the effect is punishing, and the original pain increases. The same basic message can be communicated calmly and quietly, "You can see that you must take responsibility for the broken windows. How do you want to do this?" Following are suggestions for actions that will help heal the real needs of the student.

- Repair the damage together. Since you are not trying to punish the student, you and the student may both enjoy completing the job together. This is not a suggestion to do the work for the student. The point is for the student to take responsibility.
- Say, "It's OK to be angry. It's not OK to hurt others." Explain, "Other ways to express anger are. . ." (See the section on fighting and alternatives for handling anger on page 186.)
- Hold parent conferences as quickly as possible.
- Get counseling for the student. Suggest family counseling.

Have lunch with the student for no specific reason other than to gain rapport and trust. During lunch, look at the student and listen to what she says. Do not use the time to lecture or discuss negatives about the student's behavior. You may use a metaphor. Refer to the section on metaphors on page 94.

You may be surprised how much your heart will open when you sit eye-to-eye and heart-to-heart with a troubled child. Although you cannot expect a miracle, you will make a difference, and for some children, you are the only hope they have.

Loving and understanding a child does not suggest letting her get away with inappropriate behavior. If you determine that you cannot teach and others cannot learn with this hostile child in the classroom, you will send her out of the room with compassion rather than anger.

Checklist For Challenging Children

Name of Student _____

Your Feelings: Keep a tally of the number of times you feel each way.

Hopeless   Aannoyed   Challenged   Angry

Pity for child   Hurt   Terrified   Disgusted

Behavior: Keep a tally of the number of times you notice each behavior.

Acts helpless   Says, "It's hard."   Whines

Taps pencils   Leans chair back   Interrupts

Loses items   Pulls on you   Is jealous

Defies you   Talks back   Bosses others

Is rude   Destroys things   Hurts

Steals   Fights   Uses substances

Has weapons   Implies, "I won't and you can't make me."

After tallying your feelings and the behaviors of a child for a minimum of three days, reread each behavior type to determine the underlying need and to plan your appropriate actions.

Any time your reactions to a child are not working, you must assume that you have misdiagnosed the problem.

Challenging Students Quiz

Example #1:

You are working with the class and Mary is doing her written work. Every few minutes, Mary interrupts to ask a question. Mary breaks her pencil and needs you to find a new one. She runs out of paper and asks you to help her find some. She discovers she can't remember what the assignment is. She rocks in her chair and taps her pencil on her desk.

How do you feel? What does Mary need?

What could you do to help Mary get her real needs met?

Example #2:

When the students play a game, Ben always wants to be the leader. He reads the rules and determines whether the others are playing correctly. Sometimes, he complains that no one in the class plays right. He even has to remind the teacher how to play games. When you try to talk to Ben about the game, Ben says your way is wrong and you can't make him play the wrong way!

How do you feel?
What does Ben need?
What could you do to help Ben get his real needs met?

Example #3:

Mother and Joey are shopping for school clothes. Joey has his ideas and rudely tells Mother that everything she picks out is stupid. When Mother frowns at Joey, he yells back, throws the clothes on the floor, and stomps away.

How does Mother feel?
What is really happening with Joey?
What could his mother do to help Joey get his real needs met?

Example #4:

Sue comes home with an assignment to read a chapter in social studies and answer the questions. Although Sue is a good reader and understands the social studies material, she tells her father that the assignment is too long and too difficult. When he insists that she can do the assignment, Sue cries and begs for help. Her father is tempted to do the assignment for her.

How does the father feel?
What does Sue need?
What could her father do to help Sue get her real needs met?

Some of my fondest memories in sports were a result of failure, injuries, setbacks, or mistakes. I learned far more about myself and gained more character in those difficult times than I ever did when success came easily.

~Peter Vidmar, Olympic God Medalist, Gymnastics

TURECKI'S DIFFICULT CHILD

Stanley Turecki, a family psychiatrist, and the father of an ex-difficult child, currently directs the Difficult Child Center in New York City. He has broad experience helping difficult children and their parents and he lectures extensively on family matters.

Turecki suggests that when dealing with difficult children, you need to realize the following facts.

* Difficult children are normal. They are not emotionally disturbed, or brain damaged. Difficult is not abnormal.

- Some children are difficult because of their innate makeup or temperament.
- Difficult children can become positive, enthusiastic, and creative students.

Turecki defines temperament as the natural style of behavior in each individual. According to Turecki, temperament is a genetic factor, as is hair and eye color. It determines how a student behaves, not why the student behaves as she does. How does the student respond to frustration, displeasure, boredom? Equally important, how can you react to the student's behavior in a way that promotes positive development?

Characteristics of Turecki's Difficult Child

The difficult child may display any one or a mixture of the following traits:

- high activity level, wild behavior
- distractibility
- intensity and loudness, whether happy or sad
- stubbornness
- difficulty with new people, situations
- strong reaction to sensory stimuli such as bright lights, colors, smells, pain, weather, and texture of clothes
- difficulty with changes
- moodiness with crying, and whining

Suggestions for Behaviors

Since a difficult child exhibits many inappropriate behaviors, you will find yourself constantly criticizing, correcting, and attempting to change the child unless you determine which behaviors to address and which to ignore. Turecki asks the following questions.

- Can this behavior be ignored?
- What will happen if this behavior is ignored?
- What is there to lose by doing nothing?

To determine answers to these questions, create a Relevant Behavior List. List the specific behaviors, not your attitudes or feelings about the child. After listing behaviors, determine which one, or ones you must take a stand on and consistently remain calm and firm. Ask another adult who knows the student to make a similar list and compare the two. As you and your friend read through your lists, ask one another, "Is this important?" Select one to three behaviors to target and agree to ignore the remaining behavior problems for the time being.

Together, set a goal to be practical. Plan your actions and decisions. When unacceptable behavior occurs, respond immediately with your determined plan of action.

Turecki lists several types of behaviors and suggests various responses. Each behavior will be considered below.

Highly Active Behavior

The student with wild behavior gets overly excited and loses control. Your job is to intervene early.

- Offer a cool-down area that is neither a reward nor a punishment.
- Look the student in the eye and say, "You're getting too excited. You're beginning to get wild."
- Stay neutral and calm.

Inattentive and Distracted Behavior

The inattentive student doesn't listen and tends to tune out directions and instructions. It is not as if the student is refusing to listen because she doesn't want to; rather, the student isn't listening because she has trouble paying attention. Your anger will not be helpful. Instead, you should:

- Establish eye contact.
- Say, "Look at me." Always be aware of cultural beliefs about children making eye contact with adults.
- Keep what you need to say very short.

Loud, High-Intensity Behavior

The high-intensity student is loud whether happy or sad. She constantly yells out in class and makes noises.

- Say, "I know you have a loud voice, but . . ."
- Say, "You have trouble speaking softly, but . . ."

Stubborn, Locked in Behavior

Most students can accept the fact that at times they will not get what they want. A difficult student may get locked into a desire and stubbornly refuse to release the idea. This student will continue to ask, and ask, and ask again for the same thing.

- Say, "You have asked three times. You are not going to get it."
- Say, "You may ask two more times. Then you must stop asking."
- If the student continues, ignore her.
- Teach the student to count to ten and take a deep breath.

Restless, Over-stimulated Behavior

The restless student interrupts the class. You need to determine how long she can sit still.

- Say, "I see you're getting restless. Take a break."
- If the student loses control say, "You'll do better next time."
- Teach the student to ask for a break when needed.

Difficulty With Changes

One type of difficult child cannot handle changes. It will be helpful if you prepare the student in advance by saying, "We will be putting our things away and going to lunch in ten minutes."

- Use a digital clock just for this student to let her know how long until a change will occur.
- Say, "I know it's hard to make a change."
- Say, "I know you're busy but you're getting locked in."
- Teach the student to notice the nervous feeling and to realize that the feeling will pass.
- The student may benefit from becoming a mentor to a doll or stuffed animal and assuring the doll that change will be all right.

Withdrawn and Shy Behavior

Initial withdrawal and shyness describe the student who has difficulty meeting new people and being in new environments.

- Say, "I understand this is new for you."
- Say, "It takes time to get used to a new place."

Moody, Negative Behavior

The moody student whines, cries, and complains often. This student is rarely happy and finds something wrong with every event.

- Ignore the negative attitude when possible.
- Mentally, say to yourself, *This is the way she is. It has nothing to do with me.*
- Teach the student to use positive self-talk.
- When the student insists, "I don't like it," avoid challenging the statement.
- Recognize the student's comment by saying, "I know you don't like . . ."
- Offer choices that can be answered with a yes or no.
- Insist that the student stop after responding with a simple yes or no, without telling you how much she dislikes one or both choices.

Temperament Tantrum Behavior

Sometimes a difficult student has a temper tantrum because she truly loses control. Perhaps the student's temperament has been ignored or mistreated. She becomes too frustrated and finally erupts into uncontrollable behavior. The tantrum is not designed to manipulate and the student needs assistance to change the behavior.

- Stay with the student physically, and protectively.
- Be calm and reassuring.
- Say, "I know you are upset. It will be OK."
- Use distraction if possible and avoid a long discussion.

The temperament temper tantrum tends to be more intense than the manipulative one. It will also relate to one of the student's underlying temperament issues. Your instinct will be to feel sorry for the student and to say to yourself, *She can't help this behavior and needs my help to break out of it.*

Manipulative Tantrum Behavior

A different type of temper tantrum is contrived to manipulate others. The student simply wants to get her way. Do not give in unless you believe you were being unreasonable in the first place.

- Be firm. Avoid saying, "I'm sorry."
- Say, "You cannot have . . . I want you to control yourself."
- Ignore the student if the behavior continues. Do not negotiate the issue.
- You may create a private space in your classroom for the student who has manipulative tantrums.
- Sometimes you must remove yourself and the class from the student.

The manipulative temper tantrum is usually less intense than the temperamental one. It is a result of the student not getting what she wants. The motive will be easy to determine. Your intuition may say, *She's trying to get her way with me and I cannot reward this negative behavior by giving in to her.*

What About Fighting?

If students in your classroom get into a fight, end the conflict in a way that keeps all students safe, protects you, and encourages student responsibility. Insist that there will be NO fighting in your classroom. With guidance, a conflict itself can result in a learning experience. The following guidelines create a winning resolution for you as well as the students.

- Avoid becoming the judge and jury.

- Avoid saying, "You guys drive me crazy." Students will think this is funny.

- Hold students responsible for solving their problems. Suggest, "Could you make up a new game?" or, "Is there a way you can both get what you want?"

- During a calm time, help students understand the real reason for fighting. "Could it be that you want more attention from me? Are you angry about . . .?"

- Help them realize the futility of fighting by asking them, "How do you feel when you fight?"

- Teach students to solve problems by not fighting and also not giving in. Ask, "How can everybody win in this situation?"

- If things get broken, hold both students responsible. "It isn't important who started the fight. Let's all work together to clean up the mess. How do you plan to pay for . . ."

  - Asking students to repair their damage teaches them to take responsibility. They may discover a high price tag for fighting.

  - You and their parents may choose to participate but resist the temptation to rescue them. Stay with logical consequences. Be firm without becoming angry, resentful, or punishing.

Students Who Have Behavior Disorders

Students with behavior disorders or emotional problems, suffer from internal forces that create feelings of insanity. During quiet times, the student may recall traumatic scenes or frightening events. To you, it seems reasonable to ask for quiet reflection. You want the student to think. However, every quiet, thoughtful time evokes angry or fearful images. Conflicting thoughts and feelings make it impossible for the student to think clearly.

Regardless of the cause, you must not allow disruptive behavior in your classroom. To paraphrase the words of Lee Canter, "I don't care if you are depraved, deprived, neglected, or abused. No one gets to stop me from teaching. No one gets to stop others from learning. And positive behavior will be acknowledged."

Ways to Avoid Problems

Preventing problems uses less energy than correcting them. Anderson suggests three ideas for classroom teachers who work with disturbed children.

- Give contingent reinforcement. This means, only giving rewards when a student earns them. For example, when a student enters the room courteously, smile and thank the student. If a student enters rudely, maintain a calm face, but avoid the reinforcement of your smile.

Notice what reinforces your students. What interests one student may not appeal to another.

Most students want your smiles, thumbs up, thank you, drinks of water, time to sharpen pencils, restroom breaks, computer time, lunch with the teacher, snacks, and free time. When working with difficult children, use things students want to reinforce positive behavior.

When students insist on getting tangible reinforcement for every positive behavior, say, "Sometimes, I'll thank you. Sometimes you simply get to enjoy the feeling of choosing the right action."

- Teach and constantly apply the natural laws of cause and effect. Tell students, "If ___ occurs; ___ will happen."

Cause and effect should be used for positive and negative consequences. For example, "If I signal that I want students to raise their hands, those who raise their hands will be thanked and will be called on. Those who yell out will be ignored. You choose. It's up to you."

The more the result (whether negative or positive) fits the behavior, the greater understanding the student will have.

- Never give more than one warning. Tell students what behavior you expect and what positive and negative consequences will occur based on their behavior. Wait three to five seconds. If the student has not complied by that time say, "I see you chose to . . ." (use the predetermined consequence).

Both positive reinforcement and negative consequences must be used very quickly for students with emotional disabilities.

Explain to the class that some students need more help practicing good learning behavior than others. (Always describe the learning behavior instead of talking about good and bad students. Never say a student needs help being a good girl or a good boy.)

Set up your classroom system in a way that gives every student what he or she needs to succeed. Fair does not mean treating each student the same way. Fair means giving each student what is needed for successful learning to take place.

Human beings can alter their lives by altering their attitudes of mind.
~William James

ADD & ADHD

One of your most difficult encounters will be the student with attention deficit disorder (ADD) or attention deficit hyperactive Disorder (ADHD). You will constantly wonder if she misbehaves on purpose or if she truly loses control. Even if you decide the student cannot control herself, you will want to know how to help her (and yourself) maintain balanced and rational behavior. Approximately three to five percent of the population, or two million students could be diagnosed as having attention disorders. ADD / ADHD is defined as a chronic neurobiological condition.

To identify an attention disorder, a minimum of six symptoms must be noticed for at least six months and must be evident in two or more different situations such as at home and school. Since this disorder is neurobiological, only a physician can diagnose ADD/ADHD. You, however, can assist parents and physicians by noting frequent characteristics and requesting additional testing.

Although a checklist will suggest many specific behaviors, primary types include:

- inattentive
- impulsive
- hyperactive

When left unidentified, a student with ADHD is at risk for:

- difficulty with learning
- decreased self-esteem
- challenges in social problem
- problems with family life
- substance abuse later in life

Students with ADHD are at great risk in two important areas: academic mastery and peer relations. Although ADHD is not a learning disability, it often accompanies and includes characteristics of learning disabilities. It is also not an emotional disorder. However, due to frustration, the student with ADHD often develops behavior disorders. School activities that increase the undesirable behaviors include asking the child to:

- complete tasks that are very difficult
- attend to or work on one task for an extended period
- make transitions with little or no supervision and guidance
- attend to details

Students with ADHD can learn. However, their problems with inattention and impulsivity often make learning very challenging.

Brain Function Differences

Researchers at the National Institute for Mental Health documented that students with ADHD utilize glucose, the brain's main energy source, at a slower rate than normal. Less glucose utilization manifests as a decreased ability to screen out distractions from the environment.

Imagine a filter in the brain. The purpose of the filter is to screen out excess sensory input. In most people, the filter works automatically when needed. Children diagnosed with ADHD have sluggish filters. Even when bombarded with excess noise, sights, or feelings, the filter does not do its job. The child is flooded with sensations.

Stimulants such as caffeine and drugs such as Ritalin give a boost to the sluggish portion of the brain. With the jump-start, glucose utilization improves and the child with ADHD reacts more normally in terms of attentiveness, impulsivity, and excess movement. One perplexed teacher offered a warm cup of coffee to a hyperactive child who mellowed out rather than becoming more active.

A university student convinced doctors that she needed Ritalin. Once she had the prescription, she used the pills to stay awake. This student had problems, but ADHD was not one of them.

Three Types of ADHD

To discuss the characteristics of a student you suspect has ADHD, look for and document behaviors in three separate areas. A student may demonstrate behaviors in any one area, or all three types: inattentive, impulsive, and hyperactive.

Symptoms of Inattentiveness

To identify a student who has poor attention, look for at least six of the following characteristics.

The student who has attention problems:

- cannot think in a noisy atmosphere
- frequently asks for information/directions to be repeated
- is easily distracted
- is not able to listen
- has trouble concentrating unless in a one-to-one situation
- changes activities often
- is disorganized and cannot stay on schedule
- seems slow to learn and respond (but not due to limited intelligence)
- fails to complete assignments
- turns in sloppy work
- fails to pay attention to details
- has problems maintaining attention
- fails to listen to others
- fails to finish work
- loses things
- has problems organizing tasks

The inattentive student who lacks control of impulsive and hyperactive behavior becomes the one who falls through the cracks unless you are watchful. You will notice the other two quickly and regularly!

Symptoms of Impulsiveness

Another type of student with ADHD has problems with impulsivity. Look for at least four of the following behaviors. The impulsive student:

- interrupts others
- cannot wait in line
- has trouble waiting for a turn
- blurts out answers
- talks excessively
- makes noises in class
- gets frustrated easily
- becomes very excited
- cannot adjust to new situations or schedule changes
- seems to have an internal racing motor
- feels restless
- moves hands or feet and squirms when seated

Symptoms of Hyperactivity

The student with hyperactivity creates problems at school and home. The hyperactive student will demonstrate at least four of the following characteristics. The hyperactive student:

- moves slightly even when engrossed in television or a computer game
- goes wild in crowded, busy places
- has difficulty playing with friends
- gives baby-sitters a miserable time
- makes life unbearable for substitutes
- creates chaos when shopping

- runs or climbs on things excessively
- moves constantly
- moves during sleep
- destroys and breaks things
- gets out of her seat repeatedly
- makes loud noises
- engages in purposeless behavior
- lacks appropriate goal direction

Classroom Modifications

Students with ADHD often need a multi-modal approach including educational, psychological, behavioral, and medical management.

Collaboration among professionals and parents becomes necessary. As a teacher, you want to create the most effective classroom environment possible for this student who needs order and predictability.

The key is to make modifications available to all students rather than indicating they are for students with ADHD. Students who need adaptations will use them. Others, after trial experimentation, will abandon modifications that they do not need.

Classroom Organization

The student with ADHD will do better in an enclosed, self-contained classroom instead of an open area. The following classroom ideas will help.

- Keep at least one area in the classroom quiet, calm, and uncluttered.
- Keep the environment surrounding the student as clear from distractions and movement as possible.

- Display classroom rules (maximum of five). Provide the ADHD student with a desk copy of the classroom rules.
- Post a daily schedule in the same place each day. Provide the ADHD student with a desk copy of the daily schedule.
- Create learning partners.

Classroom Management

In addition to your regular classroom management procedures, give special attention to the following ideas for students with ADHD.

- To help the child get ready for a change, offer preparation before making transitions. In some cases, a timer may help. Others respond better to a digital clock.
- Give simple and clear directions for transitions. For the ADHD student state one direction at a time. Pause between each new step in the process.
- Initially, explain, model, and rehearse procedures for every activity and transition.
- Offer regularly scheduled and frequent breaks.
- Teach students to recognize your nonverbal *time-to-work* signals.
- Establish a *secret signal* with the student to use when she is off task.
- Be positive. Tell the student exactly what you want.
- Start at a level at which the student will succeed. You can't fix every behavior at once. Ask yourself, "What is the most important behavior to alter?"
- Use consequences for behaviors that the student can control. Punishing for inattention, impulsivity, or hyperactivity will probably not increase competence.

- Set realistic expectations.
- Avoid asking the student with ADHD a question when she is off task. Instead use proximity to avoid embarrassment and help with self-esteem.
- Use physical contact such as a hand on the shoulder to redirect the student.

Modifying the Curriculum

Your goal is for all students to learn. For the student with ADHD to be available for attending and concentrating, make the following modifications.

- Reduce the amount of work. Children with ADHD do not learn better with longer tasks or assignments.
- Allow more time for the completion of assignments. Extra time may be needed to continually refocus.
- Mix some high-interest items with those that are not as fascinating to the student.
- Encourage the student to use a word processor for written assignments.
- Teach in three modalities (visual, auditory, and kinesthetic). For example, state directions, write them on the chalkboard, and model exactly what children are to do.
- Color-code all notebooks, homework folders, and assignments by using separate colors for each content area. If possible, cover texts in colors that correspond with notebooks and folders. At the least, place a corresponding-colored dot on the spine of textbooks.
- Make small, portable carrels available to all students who prefer to study on the floor. Carrels can be referred to as private offices for students.

- Offer lessons on organizing desks, packing backpacks, and storing supplies. Teach the ADHD student to place books in desks and backpacks in the order in which each subject occurs.
- If a locker is used, separate morning books from afternoon books.
- Ask your district to make the World Wide Web available to your students. For the student with ADHD, navigating cyberspace comes easily and encourages communication and socialization.
- Give tests in separate, quiet areas.
- A kind study partner may be helpful.

Modifying Homework

One of the most stressful events for families with ADD/ADHD children is the completion of homework. Reports from parents indicate tears, tantrums, frustrations, and hours of misery. Knowing how critically important a stable, happy home can be to any child, you will want to be part of the solution, not part of the problem. Consider the following modifications when assigning homework.

- Provide an extra set of books for the student to keep at home and encourage the student to highlight and annotate the books.
- Help the student organize names and telephone numbers of classmates who are willing to be of assistance.
- Be certain that the child understands the assignment by asking clarifying questions such as "Tell me exactly what you will do for this assignment."
- Be certain the child has a strong mastery of the skills and concepts involved with the assignment. You are the teacher. The parent's job is to encourage and reinforce what you teach. A parent is not the child's academic teacher.

- Help the ADD/ADHD child write the assignment in a homework folder. You may want to include your phone number and email address in case a parent needs your help.

- After observing the child in class, you will know how much work your ADD/ADHD student can complete within a given period. Adjust the homework assignment accordingly.

- Reduce the amount of homework by allowing the child to complete all the odd or all the even-numbered items. Allow the child to answer seven out of ten questions.

- Instruct parents to promote frequent breaks. Help parents determine the best location for the child's study area.

- Suggest limiting the total amount of time for homework (including breaks) to one hour. After an hour, encourage parents to allow the student to stop. Grade what the student has completed. Only if the child has done much less than you know he can do in class, expect him to spend a small part of his free time completing the assignment.

Parent support groups are available in most districts. Check the resources listed at the end of the text.

Noncompliance or Inability?

You may wonder, *How will I know if a student is causing problems because of a neurological disorder or because the student is being non-compliant?*

Any time you notice a student behaving unacceptably, tell the student exactly what you want the student to do. If the student's feet are on the desk, it will not be enough to say, "Get your feet off the desk." You must say, "Put your feet on the floor under your desk."

If the student immediately responds but, in a few minutes, forgets and puts her feet back on the desk, the student is probably reacting to temperament or neurological problems.

On the other hand, if the student grumbles about your request, asks why, or refuses to comply, the student is non-compliant. Knowing the difference helps you know when to simply remind the student again, and when to take a stand concerning negative and unacceptable behavior.

Reaction to Noncompliance

What do you do if a student, possibly with pathological disorders, refuses to comply with a request such as to go to time-out? Consider the following suggestions.

First, ask the student to go to time-out. If the student refuses to move, break eye contact and continue teaching the other students.

The student must decide: to go or to test you.

Initially, offer no reaction.

Look back at the student and say, "I can't start the two minutes until you get there." Immediately look away and continue teaching.

With your peripheral vision, watch the student. (If you believe in praying, do so silently.) The instant the student begins to move toward time-out, move to get the timer.

If the student grumbles or complains on the way, ignore the sounds. If the student moves to time-out, consider the experience a success.

If the student continues to refuse to go, you may need to gently assist her. A quick hug may help. Gathering the student's books will reduce the resistance.

Avoid a physical struggle. Say, "I refuse to force you to move to _____. If you continue to refuse, I will go to the telephone and request assistance. Help will come and you will be forcefully moved out of my classroom. You decide."

Be aware that any time you enter a student's personal space, you have crossed a boundary, and the student may retaliate.

If you get too close to a student and get hit or kicked, do not punish this aggression. Each student has a personal space that determines how close is close enough. The space around each individual creates a profound boundary issue. Enter with awareness and understanding.

Laws and Modifications

Two federal laws officially recognize ADD/ADHD as a neurobiologically based, disabling condition.

- Individuals with Disabilities Education Act IDEA is the 1995 revised version of 94-142, the legislation that created dramatic changes in special education in the 1970's.
- Section 504 of the Rehabilitation Act of 1973 This act is called the Americans with Disabilities Act and is referred to as (ADA).

Even if a student is not classified in special education, she is still entitled to services under 504. Although there are no 504 classes, every district must have a 504 coordinator who monitors classrooms to make certain appropriate modifications and adaptations are used in regular education. Your district's 504 coordinator also presents workshops explaining ADA and suggesting ways to meet the needs of children.

Please note various resources for families of children with ADD/ADHD found in the Bibliography.

He who smiles rather than rages is always the stronger.

~Japanese Wisdom

Deep in the soul, below pain,
Below all the distractions of life,
Is a silence vast and grand — an infinite ocean
of calm, which nothing can disturb;
nature's own exceeding peace;
which "passes understanding".

~R.M. Bucke

THE EXPLOSIVE CHILD

Before an emphasis on including as many students as possible in regular education, most of the children with severe behavior problems were relegated to special education teachers. In the past, children who were labeled ED (emotionally disabled) were usually educated in ED classrooms most of the day. Those with less daunting labels spent most of the day in special education with a small percentage of their time in a regular classroom.

Inclusion has become a dominant factor in education. Various school administrations interpret inclusion differently.

Some believe all children benefit from total inclusion which means the inclusion of all disabilities. Others follow a more conservative point of view and integrate those with less severe disabilities. A few consider each child individually, rather than by label, when determining the most productive learning environment. Regardless of interpretation, you are more likely to have children with severe behavior problems in your classroom than ever before.

Never have Lee Canter's words been more appropriate than today. Canter maintained that no student could stop others from learning, and no student could stop him from teaching. Positive behavior would be acknowledged. Consider using Canter's theory as a foundation for your behavior management plan.

Ross Greene's book *The Explosive Child* lists several types of children who are prone to inflexible, reactive behavior.

Who Are Explosive Children?

According to Greene, explosive children come with a variety of psychiatric disorders:

- ODD (oppositional-defiant disorder)
- ADHD (attention-deficit/hyperactivity disorder)
- Tourette's disorder
- Depression
- Bipolar disorder
- Nonverbal learning disability

- Sensory integration problems
- Asperger's disorder (a type of autism)
- OCD (obsessive-compulsive disorder

Descriptions related to the labels listed above include:

- Temper tantrums
- Mood swings
- Verbal and physical aggressiveness
- Noncompliance
- Inflexibility

Regardless of the label, the children Greene calls "inflexible explosives" need a mental script to help them avoid what he calls meltdowns. Many of the scripts suggested by Turecki beginning on page 139 correspond to the recommendations made by Greene.

Both of these experts suggest that some children cannot think clearly or stay calm in the middle of a conflict. A conflict may be as insignificant as changing subjects or sharing a game. The explosive child becomes upset over a trivial issue, gets stuck in his position, and erupts into a meltdown tantrum.

Greene recommends the following:

- Think through priorities. What is important and what can be ignored?
- Learn to identify the signals indicating that a child is headed toward disaster. Usually, it is easier to avoid a conflict than to correct one.
- Identify the situations that often trigger problem behavior.

Baskets A, B, and C

Greene recommends mentally conceiving three baskets: A, B, and C. Basket A contains behaviors that must be maintained for the safety and well-being of the child and others. From your point of view, basket A must also include behaviors that stop others from learning or prevent you from teaching. Basket A holds very few, nonnegotiable items. If upholding them involves a meltdown, you must brace yourself for the storm and call for help. Refer to actions to take in a crisis for the hostile child on page 141.

Basket B holds behaviors that are not important enough to endure a meltdown. They are important, however, and are used to teach the explosive child a new way to think and act in a crisis. Basket B issues are those that require a mental script to guide the child to a calmer state of mind.

According to Greene, the first step toward avoiding a meltdown is empathy, which sounds very much like Active Listening on page 45.

Sample Script

Teacher:"I can tell you want to continue playing the game."

Child: "It's not fair to make me stop now."

Teacher: "You're feeling upset."

Child: "Yes!"

Teacher: "Do you know what the word "solution" means?"

Child: "Is it like an answer to a problem?"

Teacher "Yes. Do you think we can find a solution together?"

Child "Maybe."

Teacher: "You want to play the game longer. I want you to get started on your math. How about you take five more minutes to play the game and then stop?"

Child: "How about 20 minutes?"

Teacher: "Well, I'm not willing for you to take 20 minutes. What would you think about 10 more minutes to play?"

Child: "OK."

Teacher: "And then you will be willing to do your math. Right?"

Child: "Right."

In the classroom, you must determine when going through a mental script holds value for all children and when you must hold the conversation in private. Keep in mind that if, in addition to having a temperament that might explode, the child also feels a need to take control. "You may decide to have the conversation away from the other children." Refer to the control child on page 143.

Basket C holds issues that you once thought were important. As you develop your priorities, you realize the issues are not important enough for a meltdown. They are not even important enough to take time to work through a mental roadmap with the child. Examples of issues in basket C include:

- Whether to wear a coat at recess
- What the child eats (unless the child has an eating disorder)
- Where to study

You will determine what goes into Basket C. If you keep very few behaviors in Basket A, you will experience fewer meltdowns. Less items in Basket B means taking less time from your class to help the explosive child think through a situation. Too many issues in Basket C may feel like chaos. After living with the baskets for a few weeks, you have the prerogative to rearrange issues. If you decide to do so, you must communicate your change of expectations to the child.

You gain strength, experience, and confidence by every experience where you stop to look fear in the face . . . You must do the thing you cannot do.

~Eleanor Roosevelt

We can always perceive others as either extending love or giving a call for help.

VIOLENT STUDENTS

Every teacher hopes for pleasant and compliant students who come to school wanting to learn. Usually, this happens. Most students do want to learn, get along with peers, and please the teacher.

What about the students who, for reasons beyond your control, come to school resisting learning, resenting peers, and defying your authority? You may face students who do not seem to respond to praise, differential reinforcement, tokens, threats of punishment, or suspension. Students who "turn off and tune out" are potential powder kegs waiting to blow in your classroom. Along with all your other responsibilities, you must keep your students and yourself safe from any potential explosions.

Violence Toward the Teacher

Students may express violence toward one another or the teacher. Violence toward the teacher occurs in one of two ways: the teacher as a bystander gets in the middle of an angry scene, or the teacher provokes anger, and the situation escalates out of control.

Students with pathologically violent tendencies hurt others. Usually, someone or something damaged these students before or during birth. Other children failed to bond during early childhood. Those who fail to bond often experience depression, have attachment issues, and tend to explode easily.

Other students become violent because of the situation. Students with ADHD, behavior disorders, and emotional disabilities may get overloaded with negative emotions and lose control. With these students, you have the greatest urgency to prevent or reduce violent behavior. There is little you can do for students with pathologically violent tendencies except document and request removal from your regular education classroom into one designed for students with emotional disabilities.

Facts Concerning Teacher Injuries

To protect yourself and to prevent violence, consider four facts about teacher injuries.

- Students with emotional fragility often overreact to teacher correction or negative experiences in the classroom. Once out of control, the students hurt a teacher by hitting or kicking.
- A surprisingly large number of violent students attend school at the elementary level. The problem begins before the upper grades.

- Most violent students (57%) are special education students. Often the students become violent with the regular education teacher after returning from special classes.
- Confrontation by the teacher precedes most violent episodes at school. Knowing how to prevent confrontation provides you with your strongest method for maintaining a safe environment.

Steps That Lead to Violence

Teacher-invoked violence takes a series of sequential steps: misbehavior, correction, argumentation, and confrontation. Student misbehavior initiates step one. Next, the teacher corrects the student. Then, argumentation becomes the third step. Consider the following examples of the first three steps.

- The student misbehaves by talking to a friend during class.
- The teacher corrects the student.
- The student says, "I'm not talking."
- Teacher: "I heard you."
- Student: "She was talking to me. It's not my fault."
- Teacher: "Don't talk back to me."

The argument escalates into confrontation.

- The teacher, with an angry look, says, "Leave the room."
- Student, with an equally angry look, indicates a refusal to leave.
- Teacher: "Don't make me come over to your desk."
- Student body language indicates, *I won't leave, and you can't make me.*
- The teacher moves into the student's space. Violence erupts.

Breaking the Cycle

At any one of the four stages that precede violence, you have an opportunity to redirect the events. Breaking the pattern before it becomes a step in the cycle becomes your number one goal.

Minimize Misbehavior

Minimize misbehavior by using the powers of proximity and nonverbal communication. Talk less and move more. The average teacher makes between 500 and 900 corrections in one teaching day. Avoid oral corrections as much as possible.

Correcting Misbehavior

When you decide to correct behavior, use proximity to move closer to the student as you continue teaching. Approach without appearing to look at or pay attention to the student.

- Stay long enough for the student to become engaged in the learning task.
- If the student self-corrects the behavior, use positive reinforcement.
  - With younger students, whisper a thank you.
  - Older students respond well to thumbs up or a smile from you.
- Vary the proximity range depending on the age and disposition of the students.
  - Appropriate proximity for kindergarten includes touching.
  - For elementary students, move within an arm's length.
  - Secondary students require more personal space. Move within approximately one body length.
  - With all students, avoid getting in their faces.

- When working with students who have emotional problems, get closer when giving assistance and instruction and stay farther away when correcting misbehavior.

Argumentation

Verbal corrections lead to argumentation. Avoid the natural inclination to get louder when a student begins to explain, excuse, or argue about the behavior you are correcting. As you get louder, the student gets louder also. Getting loud and close to a student with ADHD will easily set off undesirable behavior.

If you feel you must orally correct a student, do so in a whisper that breaks the spiral leading to violence. The student will automatically match your whisper by whispering back. This type of copying is called volume matching and is a neurological response. Even if the student argues with you, it will be in a quiet voice.

Corrections and voice volume intimidate some students more easily than others. Even those who live in homes in which yelling is expected respond poorly to loud voices. Good teachers whisper. They do not yell.

Confrontation

Avoid negative eye contact. Staring angrily at a student with your arms folded invites student violence. Remember that some cultures, Asian, Hispanic, and Native American, teach children that making eye contact with an adult is disrespectful. Do not insist that a student look at you.

One of the strongest predictors of violence is a glazed, fixed-eye stare from a student. If you see this look on the face of an angry student, immediately get at or below the student's eye level. Sit down if possible and say, "I understand. You are upset." By getting below the student, you remove the threat and communicate that you do not want confrontation.

Summary

Teacher behaviors that exasperate student violence include:

- making misbehavior a major offense
- arguing with a student
- yelling at a student
- staring angrily at the student and insisting that the student look you in the eye.

Teacher behaviors that break the spiral to violence include:

- using proximity to respond to misbehavior (kindergarten = touch, elementary = arm's length, secondary and emotionally disabled students = body length away)
- avoiding oral corrections
- quietly thanking a student who self-corrects
- refusing to argue with a student
- whispering instead of yelling
- refusing to initiate or respond to an angry stare, breaking negative eye contact
- getting lower than the student who is verging on losing control

One of your goals as an educator includes cultivating a classroom climate of love, sympathy, and understanding with the belief that ultimately, the culture of our nation will reflect the atmosphere of our schools. Can schools wait for the national climate to change? Not likely. Schools - education must set a new tone to teach and lead society at large.

Fifty years from now it will not matter what kind of car you drove, what kind of house you lived in, how much you had in your bank account, or what your clothes looked like.
But the world may be a little better because you were important in the life of a child.

~Anonymous

A Request

If you believe the information contained in this book could be of use to other teachers, or anyone who works with or interacts with children, please consider leaving a short review on Amazon or any book review site. This is one of the primary ways readers learn which books may be most beneficial to them. Thank you for your consideration, and most importantly, thank you for striving to be a positive influence in the life of a child.

~Barbara

BIBLIOGRAPHY AND RESOURCES

Adrain, L. *The Most Important Thing I Know*. Kansas City, MO: Andrews and McMeel, 1997.

Boldt, L.G. *Zen and the Art of Making a Living*. NY: Penguin Group, 1993.

Buscaglia, L. *Living, Loving and Learning*. Thorofare, NJ: Charles B. Slack, 1982.

Canfield, J. & M.V. Hansen. *Chicken Soup for the Soul*. Deerfield Beach, FL: Health Communications, Inc. 1993.

de Mello, A. *The Song of the Bird*. NY: Doubleday, 1981.

De Porter, B. & M. Hernacki. *Quantum Learning: Unleashing the Genius in You*. NY: Dell, 1992.

Dills, R., J. Grinder, R. Bandler, J. DeLozier. *Neuro-Linguistic Programming*. Cupertino, CA: Meta Publications, 1980.

Drew, N. *Learning the Skills of Peacemaking.* Rolling Hills Estates, CA:1987.

Frandsen, B. *Diversified Teaching.* Austin, TX: Family School, 1993.

Ginott, Haim. *Teacher and Child.* NY: The Macmillan Co., 1972.

Glasser, W. *The Quality School Teacher.* NY: Harper Collins, 1993.

Gordon, T. *P.E.T. Parent Effectiveness Training.* NY: A Plume Book New American Library, 1975.

Greene, R. *The Explosive Child.* NY: Harper Collins, 2001.

Grinder, M. *ENVoY.* Battle Ground, WA.: Grinder and Associates, 1993.

-----. *Righting the Educational Conveyor Belt.* Portland, OR: Metamorphous Press, 1989.

Hunter, M. *Enhancing Teaching.* NY: Macmillan College Publishing Co., 1994.

Jensen, E.P. *Super-Teaching, Master Strategies for Building Student Success.* Del Mar, CA: Turning Point, 1988.

Johnson, S. & C.J. *The One Minute Teacher.* NY: Quill, 1986.

Kandola, Aaron. "What is NLP and What Is It Used For?" *Medical New Today.* 2024.

Kvols-Riedler, B. & K. Kvols-Riedler. *Redirecting Children's Behavior.* Gainesville, FL: INCAF Publications, 1993.

-----. *Redirecting for a Cooperative Classroom*. Gainesville, FL: INCAF Publications, 1993.

Laborde, G.Z. *Influencing With Integrity*. Palo Alto, CA: 1987.

Markova, D. *How Your Child Is Smart*. Berkely, CA: Conari Press, 1992.

Marvell-Mell, L. *Basic Techniques Book I*. Portland, OR: Metamorphous Press, 1989.

Richek, M.A. *Reading Problems: Assessment and Teaching Strategies*. Boston, MA: Allyn and Bacon, 1996.

Russo, Allison. "ADD vs. ADHD Symptoms: 3 Types of Attention Disorder." *ADDITUDE*. Sept. 4, 2019.

Sandhu, D.S. "Suggestopedia and Neurolinguistic Programming." *Journal of Accelerative Learning and Teaching*. Fall and Winter, 1994. p. 229.

Turecki, S. *The Difficult Child*. NY: Bantam Books, 1989.

Vitale, B.M. *Free Flight*. Rolling Hills Estates, CA: Jalmar Press, 1986.

-----. *Unicorns Are Real*. Rolling Hills Estates, CA: Jalmar Press, 1982.

Wallas, L. *Stories for the Third Ear*. NY: W.W. Norton & Co., 1985.

Wright, C. *Basic Techniques Book II*. Portland, OR: Metamorphous Press, 1989.

Unpublished Sources

Children and Adults with Attention Deficit Disorders. Woodbridge, NJ: Core Graphics Resources, 1994.

Associations

A.D.D. WareHouse, Specializing in products for ADD/Hyperactivity: 1-800-233-9273.

ADD Line: A Tool for Success. A newsletter discussing ADD in a positive light: 1-800-982-4028.

Association for Children and Adults with Learning Disabilities (ACLD).
4156 Library Rd.
Pittsburgh, PA 15234
(412) 881-1191

Resources for Workshops and Training

Quality School Consortium
William Glasser
22024 Lassen Strees #118
Chatsworth, CA, 91311
(818) 700-8000

Redirecting for a Cooperative Classroom
Tammy Cox
2525 Wallingwood Drive
Austin, Texas 78746
(512) 329-8806

ABOUT THE AUTHOR

Barbara Frandsen grew up in the desert of West Texas and spent most of her life as an educator. She is certified as a special education teacher and as a reading specialist, and has taught students from pre-kindergarten children with multiple learning disabilities through pre-service teachers at St. Edward's University. She has also developed curricula and teaching models for student teachers and authoed several books on the subject. In the process, Barbara raised her own children.

Through years of teaching and parenting, Barbara faced the mystery of how to create mentally and emotionally healthy children. Though she retired in 2013, becoming a grandmother and great-grandmother deepened Barbara's commitment to the well-being of all children.

Follow her writing at https://barbarafrandsen.substack.com/ or contact her by email at barbarafrandsen@icloud.com.

OTHER BOOKS
BY THE AUTHOR

Parenting with Kindness & Consequences

The perfect combination of child-development research and grandmotherly wisdom. . . a practical roadmap for raising a child in the 21st century. ~Kirsten Brunner, LPC, co-author of The Go-To Guide for New Dads
Being a good parent is the most challenging—and meaningful—job anyone can assume. The manner in which parents and other caregivers fulfill this task will impact the future of the child, as well as the world. Learn to nurture children from birth, with many examples and tips on how to compassionately guide them through each stage of development. (Tranquility Press, 2022)

Slaying the Dragons: 21st Century Literacy

We know that those fearsome, fire-breathing creatures known as dragons do not truly exist. Yet, in the world of literacy instruction, teachers and parents often feel as though they are battling equally severe and frightening conditions that hinder literacy success. *Slaying the Dragons:*

21st Century Literacy considers several causes of literacy failure. The most severe challenges come from various types of dyslexia and dysgraphia and are the predominant challenges considered for remediation. Research information, suggested strategies, and recommended modifications follow the introduction of each "dragon." (Author House, 2011)

Yes! I Can Teach Literacy

Have you ever considered what a miracle it is to master reading? One school superintendent stated, "Teaching reading IS rocket science!" For those who wonder how to facilitate the miracle of converting a non-reader into a fluent one, *Yes! I Can Teach Literacy* is the book for you. Topics include assessment of reading and writing, developmental stages, emerging literacy, strategies for teaching reading, writing, and spelling, suggestions for helping children with dyslexia and dysgraphia, and specific ways to meet state objectives by using good pedagogy. At the end of the book, the generalizations of our English language are covered. (Family School Publications, 2001)

Making a Difference for Students with Differences

Whether you teach in a public, private, or a home setting, you will sometimes face the challenge of a student who learns differently. As you strive to meet the needs of a special student, you will yearn for adaptation and modification ideas. *Making a Difference for Students with Differences* contains a collection of adaptations. Many of the ideas come from areas of expertise outside education. For that reason, some suggestions may seem extraordinary. However, students with drastic needs require drastic responses. The text begins with the foundation and terminology of special education and proceeds with new terms for inclusion. A bibliography contains valuable resources for materials, equipment, and workshops to aid in teaching special learners. (Entercate Publications, 1998)

Diversified Teaching

All too often we fall into ruts, presenting lessons the same way day after day. *Diversified Teaching* offers a quick and easy way to teach reading/ language arts with the diversity that will maintain motivation for ages five through adulthood. Strategies provide teaching ideas for phonics, sight words, reading fluency, comprehension, writing and more. Writing frames (guides) are provided for easy copying and suggestions for modification are offered. (Family School Publications, 1994)

Dyslexia Analysis

In 1988, Sharon Smith and Barbara Frandsen established electronic checklists of characteristics for dyslexia, dysgraphia, and related disorders. Our purpose was to raise awareness of behaviors that can easily be dismissed as unimportant. Our hope was that checklists would be used as evidence to request in-depth testing by a school or diagnostician. (Education Analysis, 1988)

www.ingramcontent.com/pod-product-compliance
Lightning Source LLC
Chambersburg PA
CBHW052111020426
42335CB00021B/2719